Complete Math WORKOUT 1

Copyright © 2007 **Popular Book Company (Canada) Limited**

15 Wertheim Court, Units 602-603, Richmond Hill, Ontario, Canada L4B 3H7
E-mail: ca-info@popularworld.com   Website: www.popularbook.ca

Printed in China

 Contents

Section IV

Section I

Overview

In this section, Grade 1 students are provided with practice in comparing, sorting, and ordering objects according to one attribute such as size, height, width, and weight.

They will be coloring and copying objects as well as copying or choosing between words that describe objects, such as heavier/lighter and biggest/smallest. Minimal reading and writing skills are required.

Parents can enrich children's learning by providing them with real objects or drawings for comparing, sorting, and ordering, which help to arouse and sustain their interest in exploring and learning mathematics.

Comparing Sizes

Circle the smaller object.

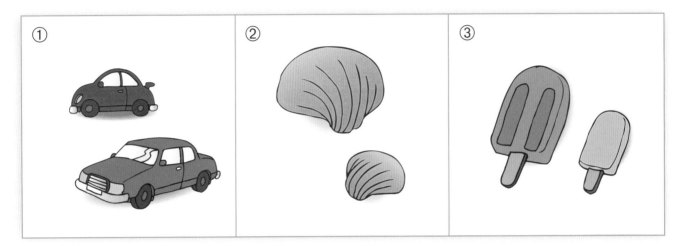

Circle the bigger animal.

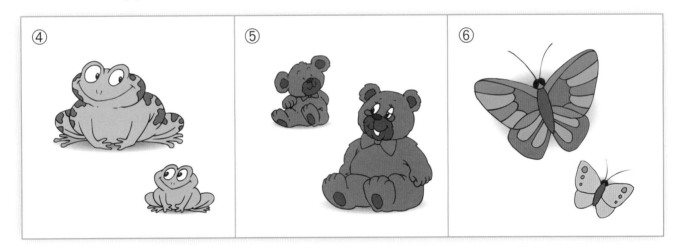

Draw a similar shape which is bigger than the one shown.

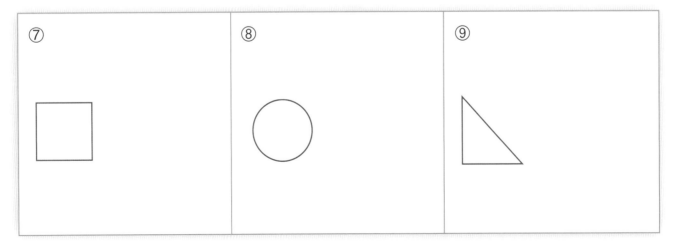

Color the container which holds more juice.

Draw a similar snack which is smaller than the one shown.

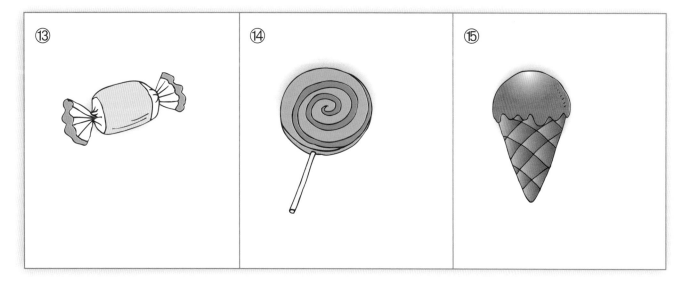

Color the biggest fruit.

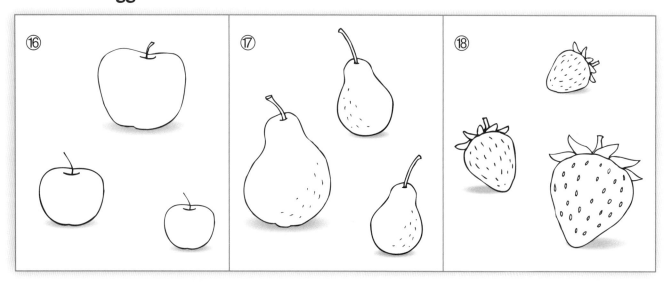

Color the smallest animal.

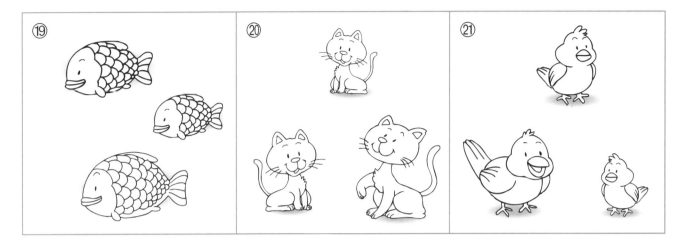

Color the container with the least water.

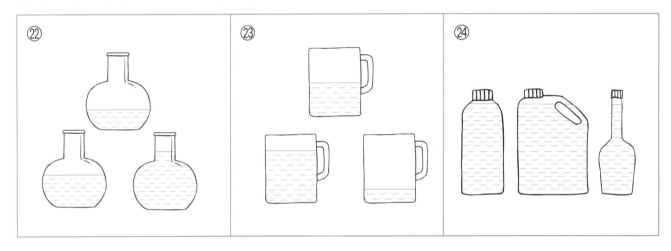

Draw lines to join the bears to their chairs.

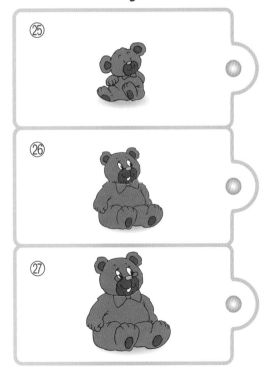
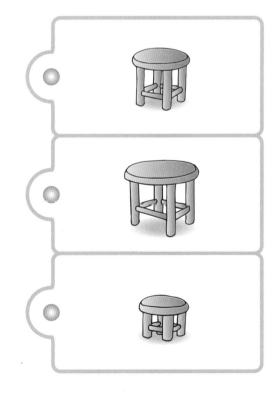

Circle the correct word in each sentence.

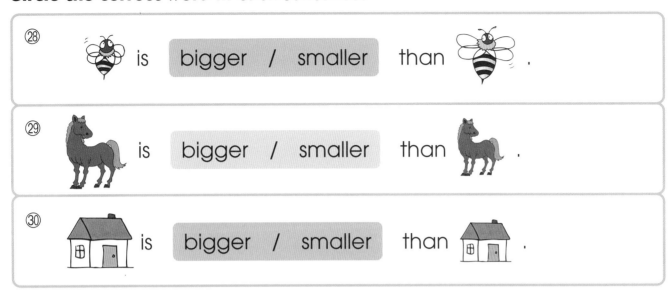

㉘   is   **bigger / smaller**   than   .

㉙   is   bigger / smaller   than   .

㉚   is   **bigger / smaller**   than   .

Look at the gift boxes. Circle the correct word in each sentence.

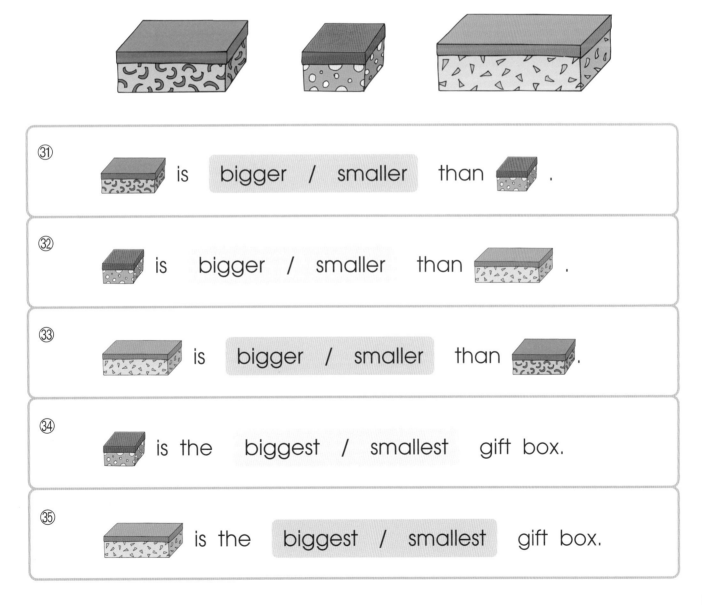

㉛   is   **bigger / smaller**   than   .

㉜   is   bigger / smaller   than   .

㉝   is   **bigger / smaller**   than   .

㉞   is the   biggest / smallest   gift box.

㉟   is the   **biggest / smallest**   gift box.

Comparing Heights and Lengths

Color the longer sausage.

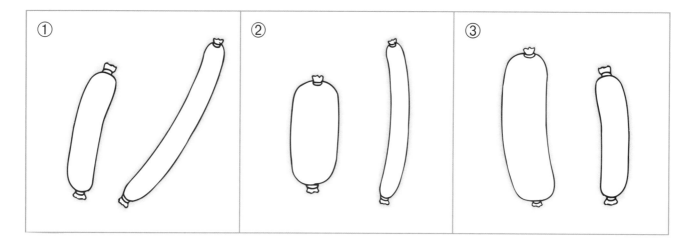

Color the shortest pencil.

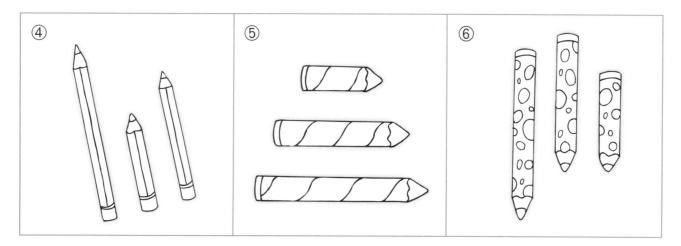

Draw a similar object which is longer than the one shown.

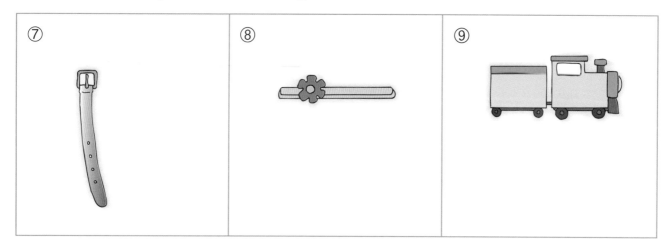

Draw a line which is as long as the one given.

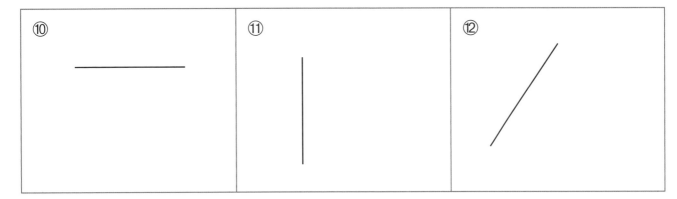

Color the taller child.

Color the tallest one.

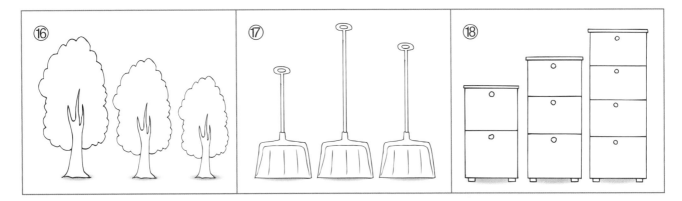

Draw a similar object which is as tall as the one given.

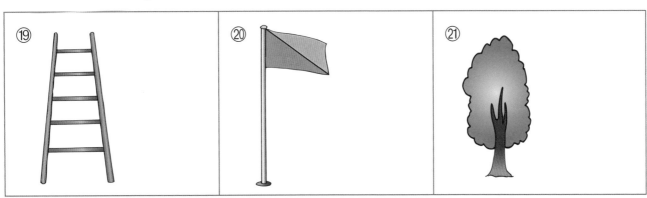

Comparing Shapes and Weights

Color the correct answers.

① Color the bread which has the thickest slices.

② Color the bottle which has the widest neck.

③ Color the sharpest pencil.

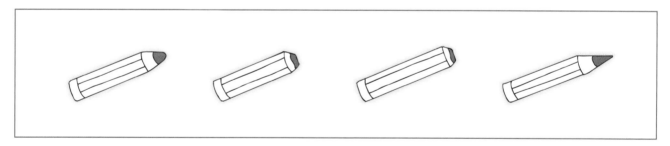

④ Color the house which has the widest pathway green and the house which has the narrowest window blue.

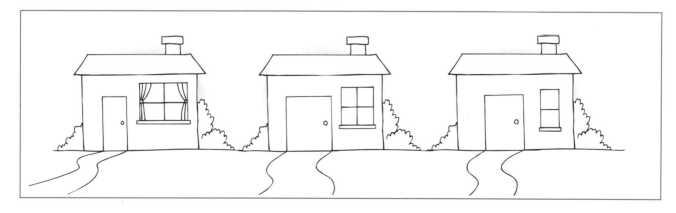

⑤ Color the thing which is flat.

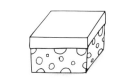

⑥ Color the thing which is hollow.

⑦ Color the thinnest book.

⑧ Color the widest shape.

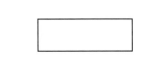  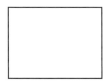 

⑨ Color the heaviest fruit.

⑩ Color the lightest thing.

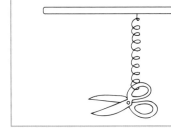  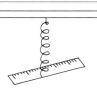 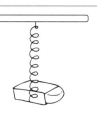

Color the heavier box.

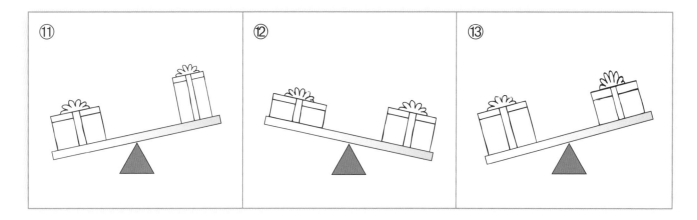

Check ✔ the correct balances.

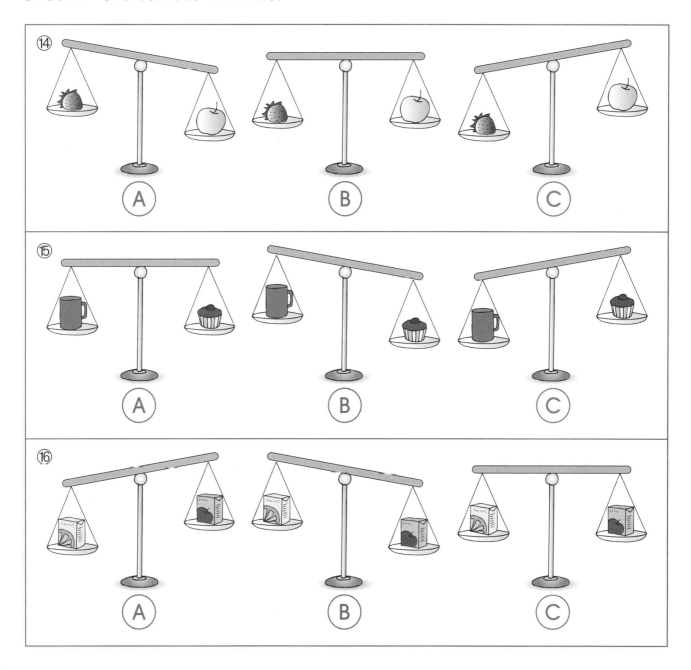

Look at the balances. Draw a picture to complete each sentence.

⑰ 🍐 is lighter than ☐ .

⑱ 🍐 is as heavy as ☐ .

⑲ 🍌 is lighter than ☐ .

⑳ ☐ is the heaviest fruit.

Look at the pictures. Circle the correct word in each sentence.

㉑ 😊 is lighter / heavier than 😊 .

㉒ 😊 is lighter / heavier than 😊 .

㉓ The ☕ is lighter / heavier than the 🍴 .

㉔ The 🪛 is lighter / heavier than the 🍴 .

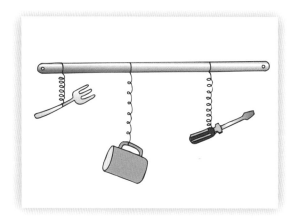

Circle the correct word in each sentence.

㉕ The opposite of light is lighter / heavy .

㉖ The opposite of heavier is lighter / heavy .

Comparing Positions

Circle the correct words.

① 🐱 is on / under the 🪑.

② 🎁 is on / under the 🪑.

③ Katie has a 🎈 in her left / right hand.

④ Katie has a 🍭 in her left / right hand.

⑤ Eva is standing on Katie's left / right .

⑥ Kevin is standing in front of / behind Katie.

⑦ 🎂 is in front of / behind Katie.

⑧ 🥄 is inside / outside the 🥣.

⑨ 🥢 are inside / outside the 🥤.

Write 'left' or 'right' to complete each sentence.

⑩ holds the with her _____ hand.

⑪ 's leash is in 's _____ hand.

⑫ The are on 's _____ .

⑬ is on 's _____ .

Write 'in front of' or 'behind' to complete each sentence.

⑭ There is a standing _____ the .

⑮ There are some standing _____ the .

⑯ The is _____ the .

Write 'over' or 'under' to complete each sentence.

⑰ is jumping _____ the .

⑱ is standing _____ the .

⑲ The is flying _____ the .

⑳ Two are _____ the .

Color the pictures. Then write the correct words.

㉑ Color the 🧸 that is inside the 📦 brown.

㉒ Color the 🪆 that is outside the 📦 green.

㉓ 🤖 is _____ the box.

㉔ Color the 🧒 that is under the ☂ yellow.

㉕ Color the 🧺 that is under the 🪑 red.

㉖ The 🐦 is flying _____ the ☂.

㉗ Color the 🧒 that is standing in front of the 🌳 blue.

㉘ Color the 🧒 that is standing behind the 🌳 orange.

㉙ The 🐕 is _____ the 🐈.

Draw the pictures.

㉚ Draw a 🍭 in Sam's right hand.

㉛ Draw a ✏ in Sam's left hand.

㉜ Draw a 🏐 inside the ▢.

㉝ Draw a 🏸 outside the ▢.

㉞ Draw an 🍎 outside the 🥣.

㉟ Draw a 🍌 inside the 🥣.

㊱ Draw a 🏐 under the ⬛.

㊲ Draw a 🕊 flying over the 🏠.

㊳ Draw some 🌸 in front of the 🏠.

㊴ Draw a 🌳 on the left of the 🏠.

Matching and Arranging Objects

Write the correct word to complete each sentence.

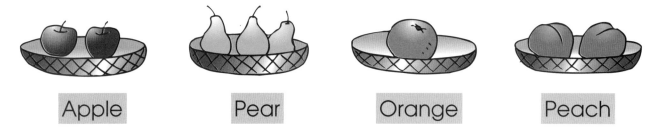

Apple   Pear   Orange   Peach

① There are more apples than _____ .

② There are fewer apples than _____ .

③ There are more pears than _____ .

④ There are as many apples as _____ .

Look at the stickers. Draw the pictures to complete the sentences.

⑤ There are more ( ) than ( ) .

⑥ There are fewer ( ) than ( ) .

⑦ There are more ( ) than ( ) .

⑧ There are fewer ( ) than ( ) .

Look at the pictures. Put a check mark ✔ in the correct circle to complete each sentence.

⑨ There are more 🔨 than ◯ ⭐ ◯ 🪣 ◯ 🐚 .

⑩ There are fewer 🪣 than ◯ ⭐ ◯ 🔨 ◯ 🐚 .

⑪ If Joe takes 1 🔨 away, there are as many 🔨 as

◯ ⭐ ◯ 🔨 ◯ 🐚 .

Look at Joe's balloons. Circle the correct word to complete each sentence.

⑫ There are   more / fewer 🎈 than 🎈 .

⑬ There are   more / fewer 🎈 than 🎈 .

⑭ There are   more / fewer 🎈 than 🎈 .

Put each group in order. Write the letters only.

⑮ From the bunch with the most flowers to the one with the fewest :

_____ , _____ , _____ , _____

⑯ From the 🧺 with the fewest apples to the one with the most :

_____ , _____ , _____ , _____

⑰ From the biggest to the smallest :

_____ , _____ , _____ , _____ , _____

⑱ From the smallest to the biggest :

_____ , _____ , _____ , _____ , _____

Look at Jill's cookies. Circle the correct word or letter to complete each sentence. Then draw the pictures.

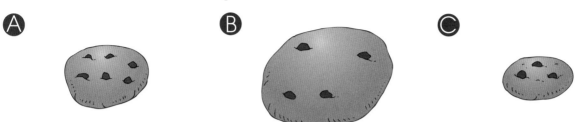

⑲ Cookie A is   smaller / bigger   than cookie C.

⑳ Cookie B is   smaller / bigger   than cookie A.

㉑ Cookie   A / B / C   is the biggest.

㉒ Cookie   A / B / C   is the smallest.

㉓ Put the cookies in order from the biggest to the smallest.

_____, _____, _____

㉔ Draw a cookie that is bigger than cookie B and with more chocolate chips on top.

㉕ Draw a cookie that is smaller than cookie A and with fewer chocolate chips on top.

Color the things. Then write the letters to put them in order.

 A   B   C   D

①   a.   Color the biggest fruit yellow and the smallest red.

     b.   From the biggest to the smallest: ____, ____, ____, ____

A   B   C   D

②   a.   Color the container that holds the most water green and the one that holds the least blue.

     b.   From the one that holds the most water to the one that holds the least: ____, ____, ____, ____

Draw the pictures.

③ Draw a ✏ which is longer than the one shown.

④ Draw a 🚪 which is narrower than the one shown.

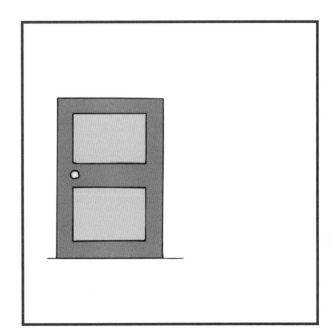

⑤ Draw a  which is taller than the one shown.

⑥ Draw a  which is thinner than the one shown.

Circle the correct words.

⑦ Jack is standing in front of / behind Lucy.

⑧ Katie is standing on Lucy's left / right .

⑨ Jack has a towel on his left / right arm.

⑩ The carpet is over / under the box.

⑪ The dolls are inside / outside the box.

⑫ The robot is bigger / smaller than the doll.

⑬ There are more / fewer dolls than robots.

25

Check ✓ the heavier object.

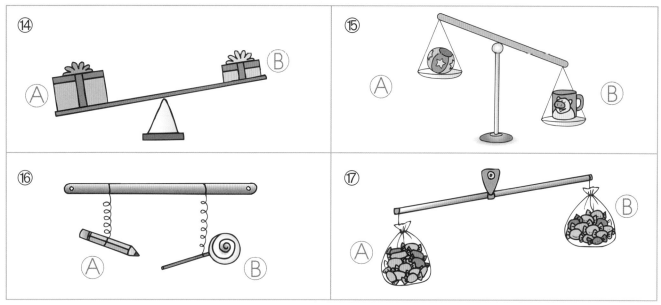

Fill in the blanks.

⑱ Jack is holding a 🍭 with his _____ left/right hand.

⑲ Betsy is holding a 🍴 with her _____ left/right hand.

⑳ Betsy is sitting on the _____ left/right of Brad.

㉑ Sally is standing _____ behind/in front of Brad.

㉒ Anne is putting a 🍽 _____ over/under Jack's head.

㉓ The 🥄 is _____ inside/outside the 🥣 .

㉔ The 🎉 is _____ inside/outside the 📦 .

Check ✓ the group which has more.

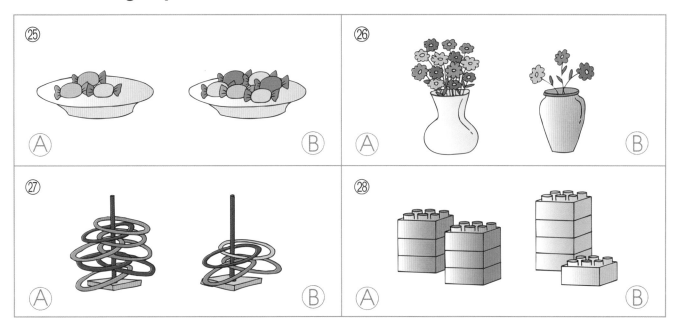

Match the muffins with the boxes. Then fill in the blanks with the correct letters.

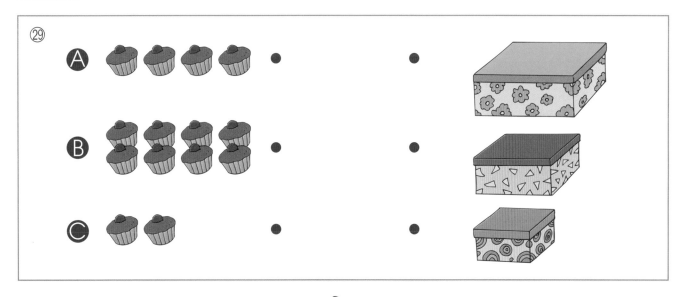

㉚ Group _____ has the most 🧁 .

㉛ Group _____ has the fewest 🧁 .

㉜ Put the groups in order from the one which has the most 🧁 to the one which has the fewest.

_____ , _____ , _____

Ordering Objects (1)

Cross out X the thing in each group which is in the wrong order.

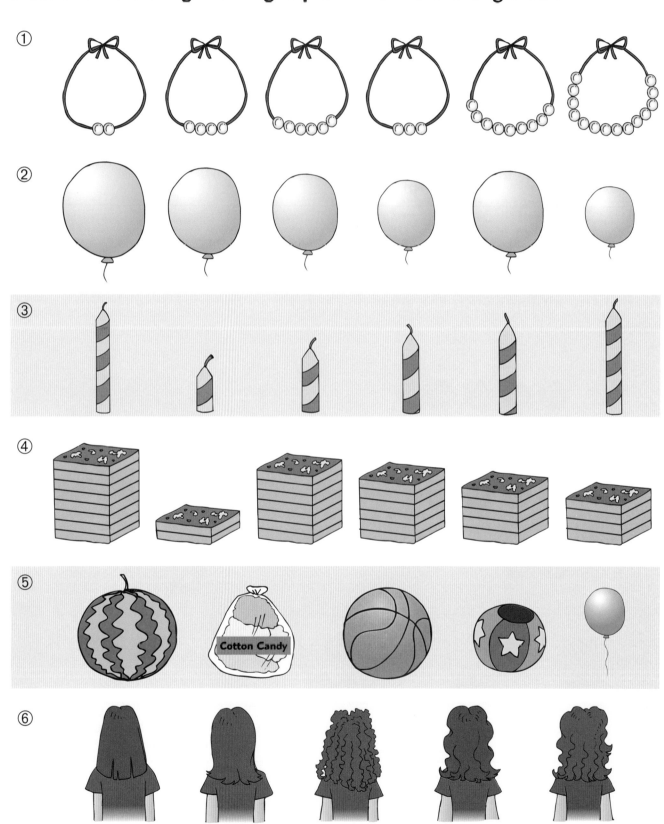

Draw lines to match the animals with their food by size.

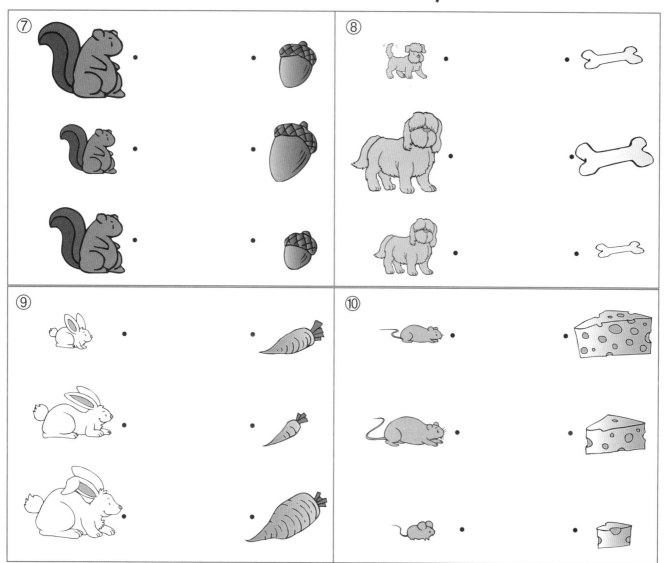

Match the things with the correct boxes. Write the letters in the circles.

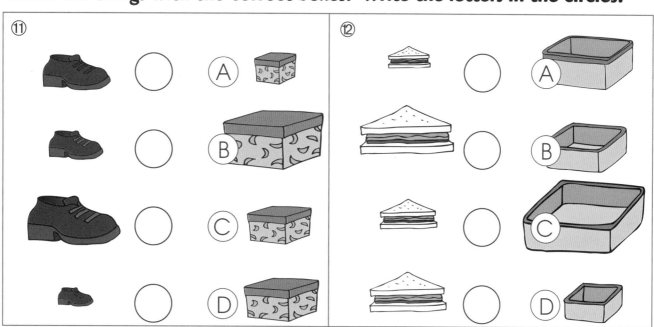

Ordering Objects (2)

Put each group of things in order. Write the letters only.

① Ⓐ Ⓑ Ⓒ Ⓓ

From the longest to the shortest: _____ , _____ , _____ , _____

②

From the thickest to the thinnest: _____ , _____ , _____ , _____

③

From the narrowest to the widest: _____ , _____ , _____ , _____

④

From the tallest to the shortest: _____ , _____ , _____ , _____

⑤

From the smallest to the biggest: _____ , _____ , _____ , _____

⑥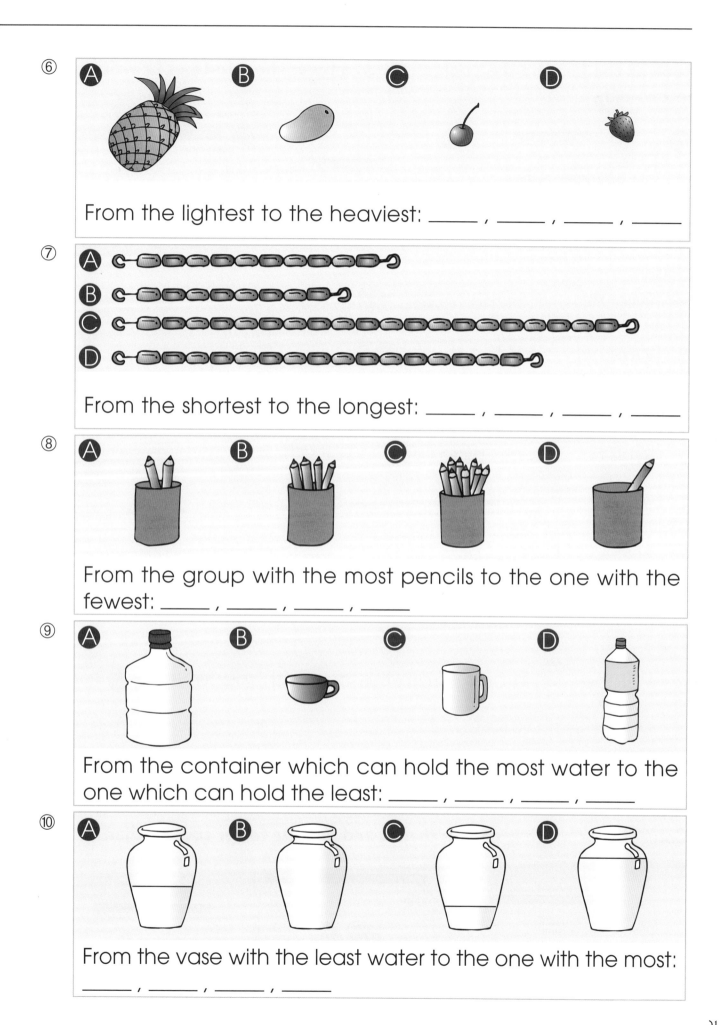

Ⓐ Ⓑ Ⓒ Ⓓ

From the lightest to the heaviest: _____ , _____ , _____ , _____

⑦

Ⓐ Ⓑ Ⓒ Ⓓ

From the shortest to the longest: _____ , _____ , _____ , _____

⑧

Ⓐ Ⓑ Ⓒ Ⓓ

From the group with the most pencils to the one with the fewest: _____ , _____ , _____ , _____

⑨

Ⓐ Ⓑ Ⓒ Ⓓ

From the container which can hold the most water to the one which can hold the least: _____ , _____ , _____ , _____

⑩

Ⓐ Ⓑ Ⓒ Ⓓ

From the vase with the least water to the one with the most: _____ , _____ , _____ , _____

Look at the jars and the cookies. Then answer the questions by writing the letters only.

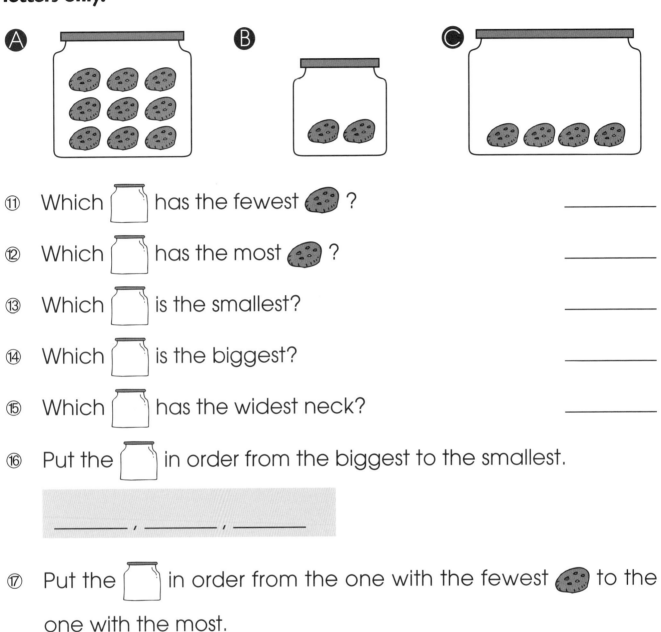

⑪ Which [jar] has the fewest 🍪 ? _____

⑫ Which [jar] has the most 🍪 ? _____

⑬ Which [jar] is the smallest? _____

⑭ Which [jar] is the biggest? _____

⑮ Which [jar] has the widest neck? _____

⑯ Put the [jar] in order from the biggest to the smallest.

_____ , _____ , _____

⑰ Put the [jar] in order from the one with the fewest 🍪 to the one with the most.

_____ , _____ , _____

Color the jar which is smaller than C and holding fewer cookies than C.

⑱

Look at the baskets of apples. Fill in the blanks and put the baskets in order.

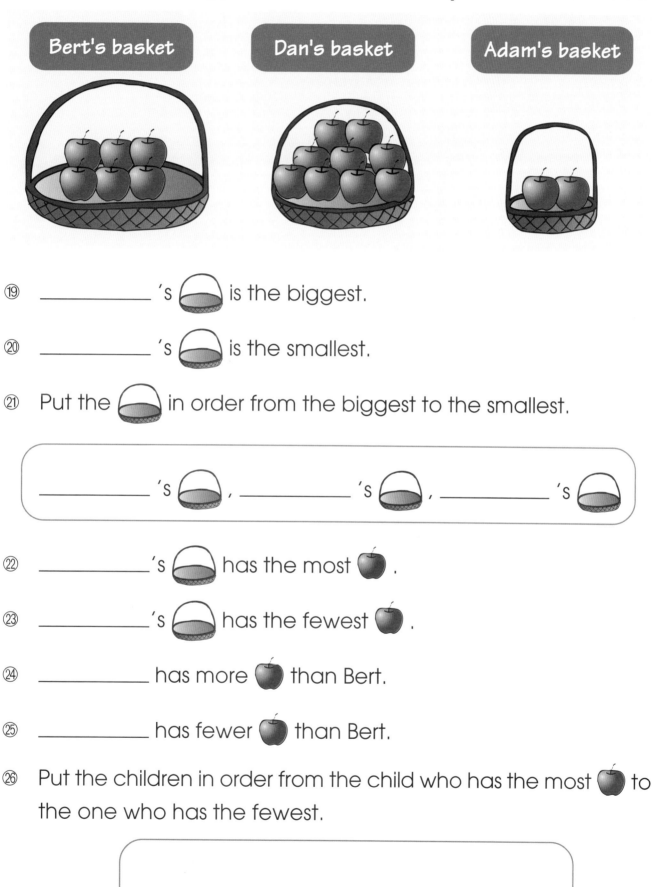

⑲ _____ 's 🧺 is the biggest.

⑳ _____ 's 🧺 is the smallest.

㉑ Put the 🧺 in order from the biggest to the smallest.

_____ 's 🧺 , _____ 's 🧺 , _____ 's 🧺

㉒ _____ 's 🧺 has the most 🍎 .

㉓ _____ 's 🧺 has the fewest 🍎 .

㉔ _____ has more 🍎 than Bert.

㉕ _____ has fewer 🍎 than Bert.

㉖ Put the children in order from the child who has the most 🍎 to the one who has the fewest.

_____ , _____ , _____

Sorting Objects (1)

Cross out ✗ the one that does not belong.

⑦

⑧

⑨

⑩

⑪

⑫

Cross out X the objects which are in the wrong place.

⑬

⑭

⑮

⑯

⑰

⑱

⑲

⑳

Draw lines to join the toys to the box and the clothing to the basket.

㉑

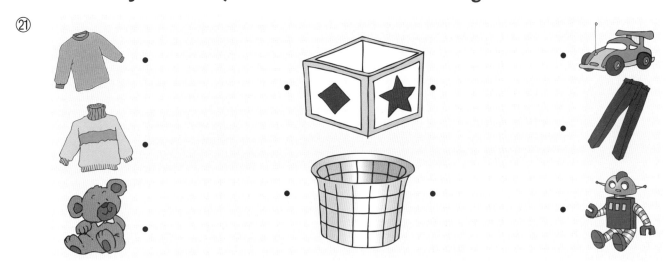

Draw lines to join the letters to the letter box and the numbers to the number box.

㉒

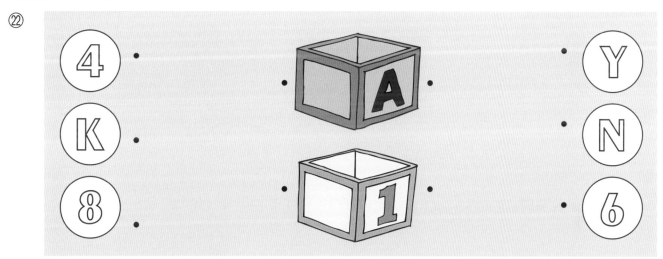

Draw lines to join the tools to the tool box and the cooking utensils to the tray.

㉓

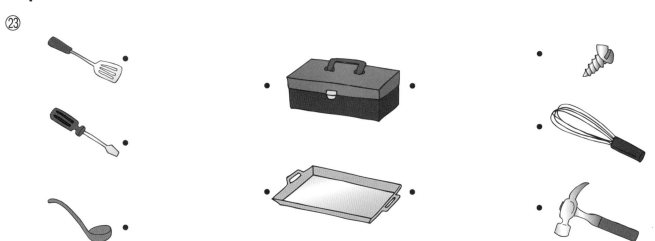

Sorting Objects (2)

Color the correct pictures.

①   Color the things you might find at a birthday party.

②   Color the animals you would find in water.

③   Color the things you might find on the beach.

④   Color the food you would put in the refrigerator.

⑤ Color the things you would put in the closet.

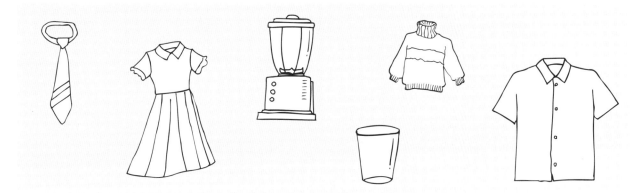

⑥ Color the things you would find in a grocery store.

⑦ Color the things you would find on a farm.

⑧ Color the things you would drink.

Sort the things. Write the letters in the boxes.

⑨

can fly	cannot fly

⑩

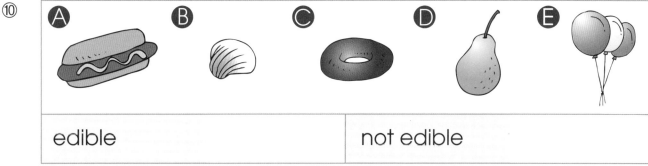

edible	not edible

⑪

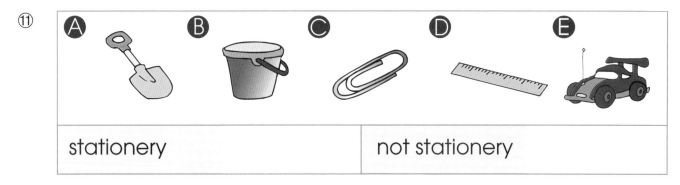

stationery	not stationery

⑫

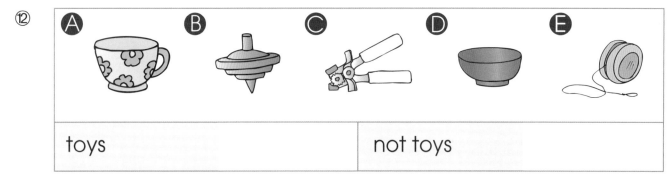

toys	not toys

⑬

animals	plants

Divide the clothing into 3 different groups. Color each group with the same color.

⑭

Divide the animals into 2 groups. Color each group of animals with the same color.

⑮

Divide the toys into 2 groups. Color each group of toys with the same color.

⑯

Final | Review

Color the thing that does not belong in each group.

①

②

③

④

Cross out X the things that are put in the wrong place.

⑤ ⑥

Color the ribbons and put them in order.

⑦   a.   Color the longest ribbon blue and the shortest yellow.

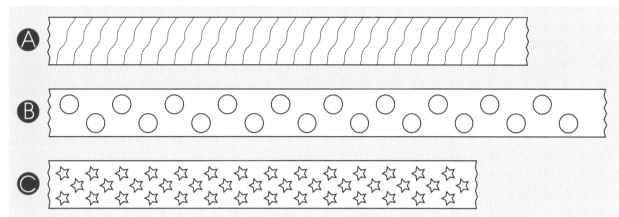

      b.   Put the ribbons in order from the longest to the shortest.

————————— , ————————— , —————————

Cross out ✗ the thing which is in the wrong order.

⑧

⑨

⑩

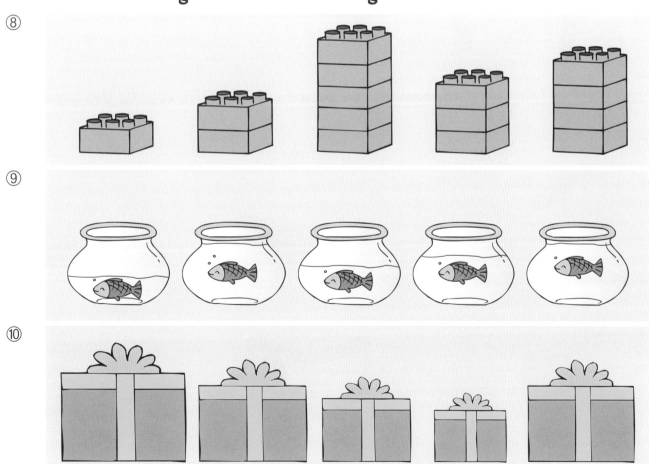

Put the things in order. Write the letters.

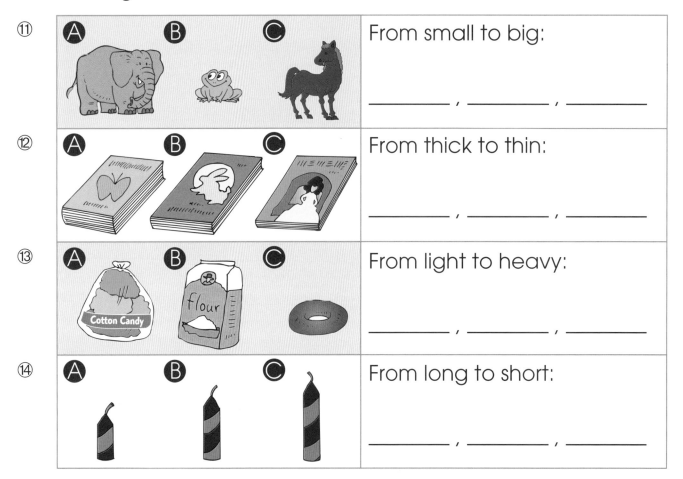

⑪ **A** **B** **C** From small to big:

_____ , _____ , _____

⑫ **A** **B** **C** From thick to thin:

_____ , _____ , _____

⑬ **A** **B** **C** From light to heavy:

Cotton Candy flour

_____ , _____ , _____

⑭ **A** **B** **C** From long to short:

_____ , _____ , _____

Draw lines to join the stationery to the pencil case and the toys to the toy box.

⑮

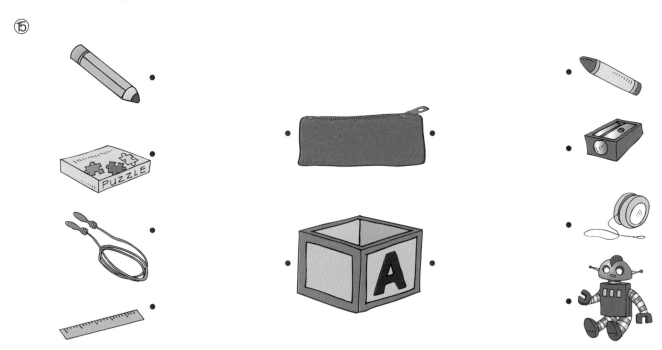

Draw lines to join the things to the correct stores.

⑯

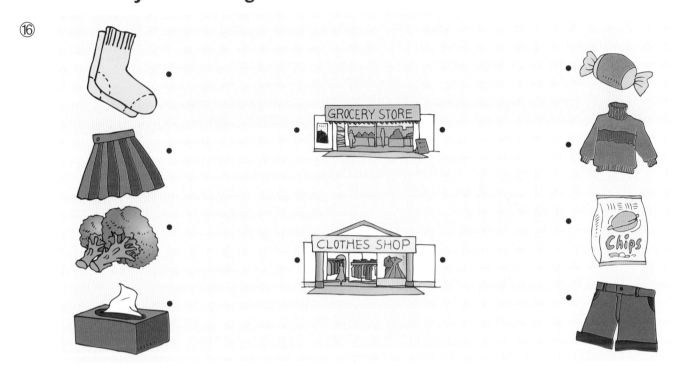

Divide the things into two groups. Color each group with the same color.

⑰

⑱

Help the bee reach the flowers by coloring the animals that have wings.

⑲

Which comes next? Circle the correct picture.

⑳

㉑

㉒

㉓

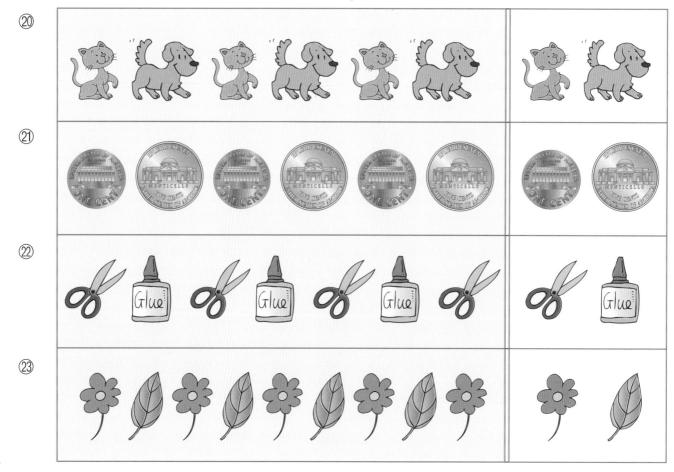

Overview

In Section I, children practiced preschool skills such as comparing, sorting, and ordering objects according to a single attribute such as size, height, and weight. They also matched objects by one-to-one correspondence and practiced counting to identify sets with more, fewer, or the same number of objects. These skills are now built upon in Section II.

In this section, children are given exercises to develop and practice the basic arithmetic skills of addition and subtraction.

Addition involves putting two groups together whereas subtraction involves taking one group from another.

Through drawing or using concrete materials, the concept of addition and subtraction is reinforced. Children learn such mathematical terms as sum, difference, total and equal, and also the signs (+, –, =) that represent these terms.

Before children make any number sentences, they must understand the quantities the numbers represent, and what happens when quantities are combined or when two groups are compared.

These skills are applied in everyday situations, using whole numbers up to 20.

Addition and Subtraction of 1

E X A M P L E S

1.    add 1 →

    3   +   1   =   4

2.    subtract 1 →

    3   −   1   =   2

HINTS:

- Adding 1 is to count 1 forward.
- Subtracting 1 is to count 1 backward.
- " + " means ADD.
- " − " means SUBTRACT.
- " = " means EQUAL TO.

Draw 1 more. How many are there in all?

①    2

②    _____

③   _____   ④   _____

Cross 1 out. How many are left?

⑤ 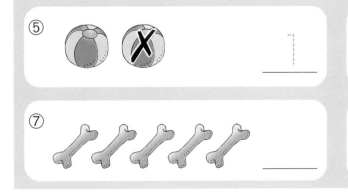   1   ⑥    _____

⑦ 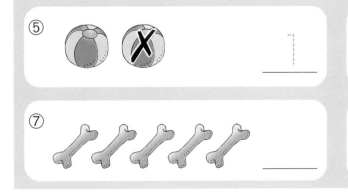   _____   ⑧    _____

How many are there?

⑨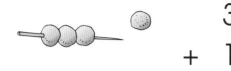

$$\begin{array}{r} 3 \\ + \ 1 \\ \hline \end{array}$$

3 + 1 = _____

⑩

$$\begin{array}{r} 4 \\ + \ 1 \\ \hline \end{array}$$

4 + 1 = _____

⑪

$$\begin{array}{r} 4 \\ - \ 1 \\ \hline \end{array}$$

4 - 1 = _____

⑫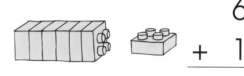

$$\begin{array}{r} 6 \\ + \ 1 \\ \hline \end{array}$$

6 + 1 = _____

⑬

$$\begin{array}{r} 2 \\ + \ 1 \\ \hline \end{array}$$

2 + 1 = _____

⑭

$$\begin{array}{r} 5 \\ - \ 1 \\ \hline \end{array}$$

5 - 1 = _____

⑮

$$\begin{array}{r} 7 \\ - \ 1 \\ \hline \end{array}$$

7 - 1 = _____

⑯

$$\begin{array}{r} 3 \\ - \ 1 \\ \hline \end{array}$$

3 - 1 = _____

⑰

$$\begin{array}{r} 8 \\ + \ 1 \\ \hline \end{array}$$

8 + 1 = _____

⑱

$$\begin{array}{r} 8 \\ - \ 1 \\ \hline \end{array}$$

8 - 1 = _____

Add or subtract.

⑲ 1 + 1 = ☐   ⑳ 2 - 1 = ☐

㉑ 2 + 1 = ☐   ㉒ 3 - 1 = ☐

㉓ 3 + 1 = ☐   ㉔ 4 - 1 = ☐

㉕ 4 + 1 = ☐   ㉖ 5 - 1 = ☐

㉗ 5 + 1 = ☐   ㉘ 6 - 1 = ☐

㉙ 6 + 1 = ☐   ㉚ 7 - 1 = ☐

㉛ 7 + 1 = ☐   ㉜ 8 - 1 = ☐

㉝ 8   ㉞ 9   ㉟ 10   ㊱ 2
  + 1   + 1   - 1   + 1
  ☐   ☐   ☐   ☐

㊲ 5   ㊳ 9   ㊴ 4   ㊵ 5
  + 1   - 1   + 1   - 1
  ☐   ☐   ☐   ☐

㊶ 4   ㊷ 3   ㊸ 7   ㊹ 8
  - 1   + 1   - 1   - 1
  ☐   ☐   ☐   ☐

Complete. Write + or − in the ◯.

㊺

_____ ◯ _____ = _____

㊼

_____ ◯ _____ = _____

㊻

_____ ◯ _____ = _____

㊽

_____ ◯ _____ = _____

Complete each number sentence. Write + or − in the ◯.

㊾ There are 8 . Buy 1 more. How many are there in all?

_____ ◯ _____ = _____   _____ in all

㊿ There are 7 . 1 is eaten. How many are left?

_____ ◯ _____ = _____   _____ left

51 There are 6 . 1 flies away. How many are left?

_____ ◯ _____ = _____   _____ left

Just for Fun

Write the missing numbers.

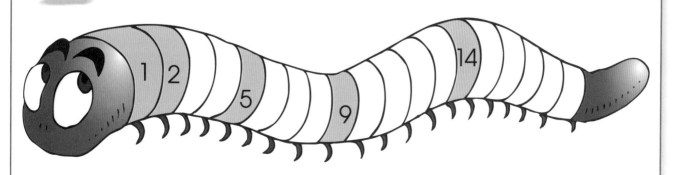

Addition Facts to 6

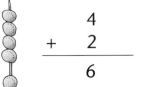

$$\begin{array}{r} 4 \\ +\quad 2 \\ \hline 6 \end{array}$$

4 and 2; 6 in all

4 + 2 = 6

HINTS:

- Vertical addition:

$$\begin{array}{r} 3 \\ +\quad 1 \\ \hline 4 \end{array}$$ ← align on the right-hand side

- Matching addition sentence:

3 + 1 = 4

Complete each addition sentence.

① ◯◯ + ◯◯◯

___2___ + ___3___ = ___5___

②

_____ + _____ = ___

③

_____ + _____ = _____

④

_____ + _____ = _____

⑤

_____ + _____ = _____

⑥

_____ + _____ = _____

⑦

_____ + _____ = _____

⑧

_____ + _____ = _____

Add.

⑨   3 + 3 = ☐   ⑩   3 + 2 = ☐

⑪   1 + 4 = ☐   ⑫   1 + 2 = ☐

⑬   4 + 2 = ☐   ⑭   2 + 2 = ☐

⑮   2 + 3 = ☐   ⑯   5 + 1 = ☐

⑰   2 + 4 = ☐   ⑱   1 + 1 = ☐

⑲   3 + 1 = ☐   ⑳   4 + 1 = ☐

㉑   1 + 5 = ☐   ㉒   1 + 3 = ☐

㉓ 3	㉔ 2	㉕ 2	㉖ 2
+ 3	+ 4	+ 2	+ 1
☐	☐	☐	☐
㉗ 3	㉘ 1	㉙ 2	㉚ 1
+ 2	+ 5	+ 3	+ 4
☐	☐	☐	☐
㉛ 1	㉜ 4	㉝ 5	㉞ 1
+ 2	+ 2	+ 1	+ 3
☐	☐	☐	☐

Match.

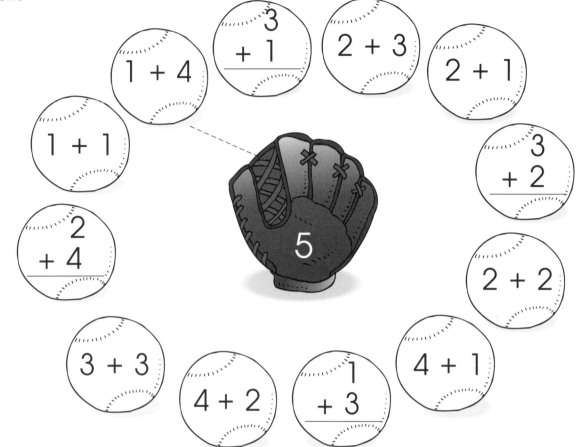

1 + 4

3 + 1

2 + 3

2 + 1

1 + 1

3 + 2

2 + 4

2 + 2

3 + 3

4 + 2

1 + 3

4 + 1

5

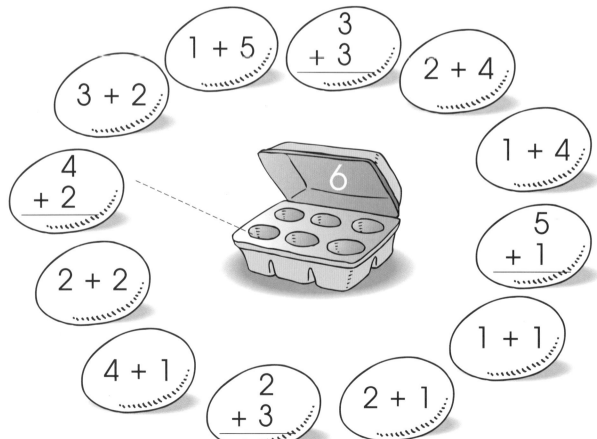

1 + 5

3 + 3

2 + 4

3 + 2

1 + 4

4 + 2

5 + 1

2 + 2

1 + 1

4 + 1

2 + 3

2 + 1

6

Color the two sets of beads that make each bracelet. Write addition sentences to match.

㊲ -OO-   -OOO-   -OOOO-   ➡️

_____ + _____ = _____

㊳ -OO-   -OOO-   -OOOO-   ➡️

_____ + _____ = _____

Complete each addition sentence.

㊴ There are 3 🍎 and 2 🍎. How many 🍎 🍎 are there?

_____ + _____ = _____   There are _____ 🍎 🍎.

㊵ There are 4 🐿️ and 2 🐿️. How many 🐿️ 🐿️ are there?

_____ + _____ = _____   There are _____ 🐿️ 🐿️.

㊶ There are 3 👒 and 3 👒. How many 👒 👒 are there?

_____ + _____ = _____   There are _____ 👒 👒.

Just for Fun

Match.

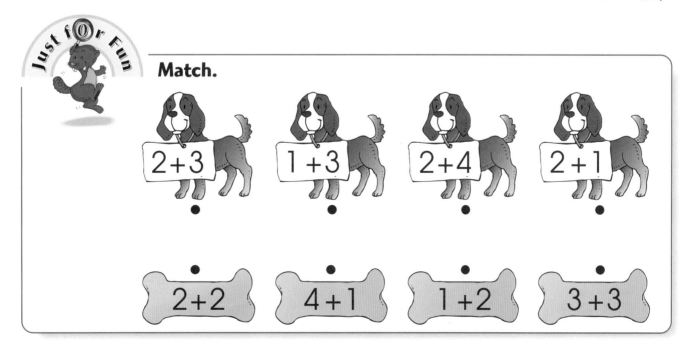

2+3   1+3   2+4   2+1

2+2   4+1   1+2   3+3

55

3 Subtraction Facts to 6

Take away 2; 4 are left.
6 – 2 = 4

$$\begin{array}{r} 6 \\ -\ 2 \\ \hline 4 \end{array}$$

HINTS:

- Vertical subtraction:

$$\begin{array}{r} 3 \\ -\ 2 \\ \hline 1 \end{array}$$ ← align on the right-hand side

- Matching subtraction sentence:

3 – 2 = 1

Complete each subtraction sentence.

①

5 – 3 = 2

②

____ – ____ = ____

③ ____ – ____ = ____

④ ____ – ____ = ____

⑤ ____ – ____ = ____

⑥ ____ – ____ = ____

⑦ ____ – ____ = ____

⑧ ____ – ____ = ____

Subtract.

⑨   4 – 2 = ☐   ⑩   6 – 1 = ☐

⑪   6 – 5 = ☐   ⑫   5 – 4 = ☐

⑬   5 – 3 = ☐   ⑭   4 – 3 = ☐

⑮   6 – 2 = ☐   ⑯   5 – 2 = ☐

⑰   3 – 2 = ☐   ⑱   6 – 4 = ☐

⑲   6 – 3 = ☐   ⑳   4 – 1 = ☐

㉑   5 – 1 = ☐   ㉒   3 – 1 = ☐

㉓ 5 – 4 ☐	㉔ 4 – 2 ☐	㉕ 6 – 2 ☐	㉖ 3 – 1 ☐
㉗ 6 – 4 ☐	㉘ 5 – 3 ☐	㉙ 4 – 3 ☐	㉚ 5 – 2 ☐
㉛ 3 – 2 ☐	㉜ 6 – 3 ☐	㉝ 5 – 1 ☐	㉞ 6 – 5 ☐

Match.

㉟

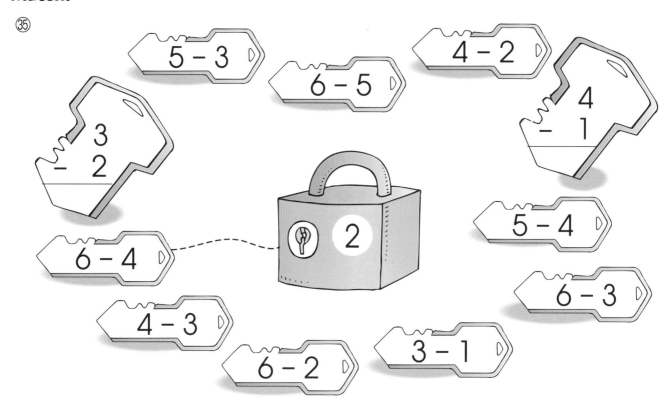

㊱

Complete each subtraction sentence.

③⑦

How many 🐦 are left?

_____ − _____ = _____

③⑧

How many 🥚 are left?

_____ − _____ = _____

③⑨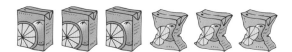

How many 📦 are left?

_____ − _____ = _____

④⓪

How many 🍎 are left?

_____ − _____ = _____

④①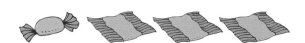

How many 🍬 are left?

_____ − _____ = _____

④②

How many 🧁 are left?

_____ − _____ = _____

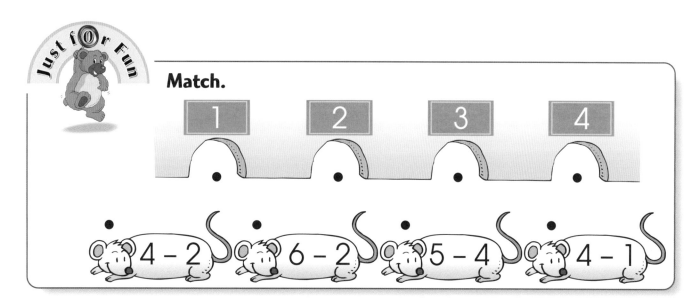

Match.

| 1 | 2 | 3 | 4 |

4 − 2   6 − 2   5 − 4   4 − 1

Addition and Subtraction of 0

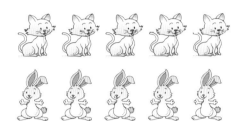

None goes.   5 – 0 = 5

None comes.   5 + 0 = 5

HINTS:

- " 0 " means NONE.
- Any number plus 0 equals itself.
- Any number minus 0 equals itself.

How many are there?

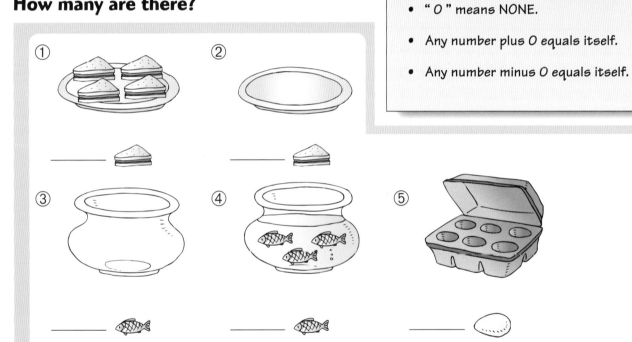

① _____

② _____

③ _____

④ _____

⑤ _____

Complete each number sentence.

⑥

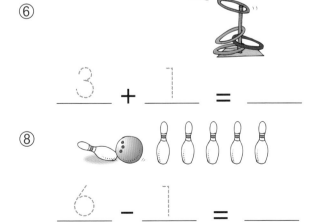

_3_ + _1_ = _____

⑦

_3_ + _0_ = _____

⑧ _6_ – _1_ = _____

⑨ _6_ – _0_ = _____

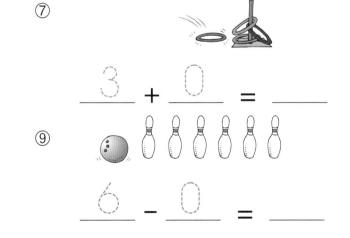

60

Add or subtract.

⑩   6 + 0 =

⑪   6 - 0 = ☐

⑫   5 + 0 = ☐

⑬   5 - 0 = ☐

⑭   4 + 0 = ☐

⑮   4 - 0 = ☐

⑯   3 + 0 = ☐

⑰   3 - 0 = ☐

⑱   2 + 0 = ☐

⑲   2 - 0 = ☐

⑳   1 + 0 = ☐

㉑   1 - 0 = ☐

㉒   0 + 0 = ☐

㉓   0 - 0 = ☐

㉔
$$\begin{array}{r} 5 \\ + \ 0 \\ \hline \square \end{array}$$

㉕
$$\begin{array}{r} 0 \\ + \ 4 \\ \hline \square \end{array}$$

㉖
$$\begin{array}{r} 3 \\ - \ 0 \\ \hline \square \end{array}$$

㉗
$$\begin{array}{r} 0 \\ + \ 1 \\ \hline \square \end{array}$$

㉘
$$\begin{array}{r} 0 \\ + \ 6 \\ \hline \square \end{array}$$

㉙
$$\begin{array}{r} 3 \\ + \ 0 \\ \hline \square \end{array}$$

㉚
$$\begin{array}{r} 0 \\ + \ 5 \\ \hline \square \end{array}$$

㉛
$$\begin{array}{r} 6 \\ - \ 0 \\ \hline \square \end{array}$$

㉜
$$\begin{array}{r} 4 \\ - \ 0 \\ \hline \square \end{array}$$

㉝
$$\begin{array}{r} 0 \\ + \ 2 \\ \hline \square \end{array}$$

㉞
$$\begin{array}{r} 4 \\ + \ 0 \\ \hline \square \end{array}$$

㉟
$$\begin{array}{r} 2 \\ - \ 0 \\ \hline \square \end{array}$$

Match.

㊱

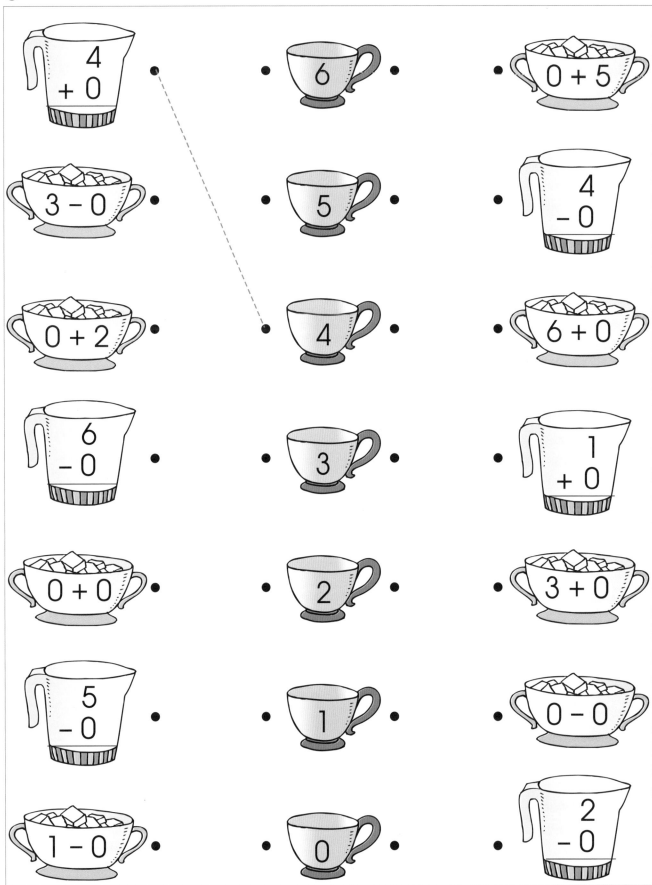

Add or subtract 0.

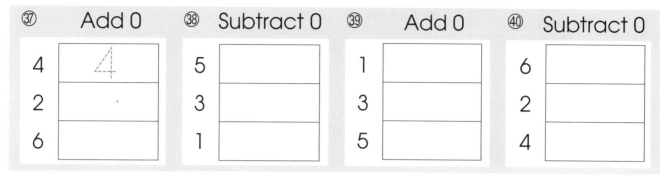

�37 Add 0		㊳ Subtract 0		㊴ Add 0		㊵ Subtract 0	
4	4	5		1		6	
2		3		3		2	
6		1		5		4	

Complete.

㊶
and

How many 🌸 are there?

$4 + 0 =$ _____

_____ 🌸 in all

㊷ 
and

How many 🐟 are there?

_____

_____ 🐟 in all

㊸ 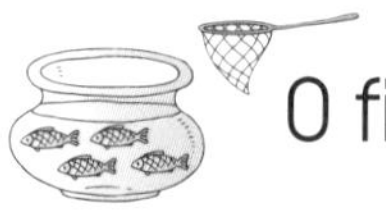 0 fish is taken away.

How many 🐟 are left?

_____

_____ 🐟 left

㊹ 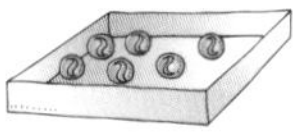 0 🎾 rolls off.

How many 🎾 are left?

_____

_____ 🎾 left

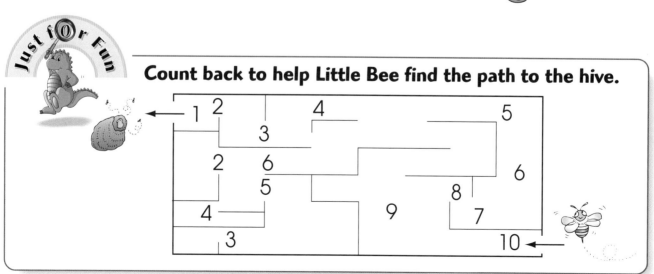

Count back to help Little Bee find the path to the hive.

1 2   4   5
      3
   2 6   6
      5   8
4 ——   9   7
   3   10 ◄

63

5 Addition and Subtraction Facts to 6

1. The sum of 3 and 2 is 5.

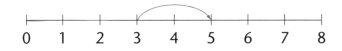

2. The difference between 5 and 2 is 3.

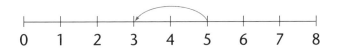

HINTS:

- Addition
  $3 + 2 = 5$ ⟵ sum

- Subtraction
  $5 - 2 = 3$ ⟵ difference

Complete each number sentence. Put + or –
in the ◯ **.**

①

$$4 \,\oplus\, 2 = 6$$

②

____ ◯ ____ = ____

③

____ ◯ ____ = ____

④

____ ◯ ____ = ____

⑤

____ ◯ ____ = ____

⑥

____ ◯ ____ = ____

Add or subtract.

⑦   4 − 3 = ☐   ⑧   2 + 2 = ☐

⑨   3 + 1 = ☐   ⑩   5 − 2 = ☐

⑪   4 + 2 = ☐   ⑫   6 − 3 = ☐

⑬   3 + 3 = ☐   ⑭   3 + 0 = ☐

⑮   1 − 1 = ☐   ⑯   4 − 2 = ☐

⑰   5 − 3 = ☐   ⑱   2 + 1 = ☐

⑲   6 − 2 = ☐   ⑳   2 + 3 = ☐

㉑
$$\begin{array}{r} 5 \\ + 0 \\ \hline \end{array}$$
☐

㉒
$$\begin{array}{r} 6 \\ - 5 \\ \hline \end{array}$$
☐

㉓
$$\begin{array}{r} 4 \\ - 0 \\ \hline \end{array}$$
☐

㉔
$$\begin{array}{r} 2 \\ - 1 \\ \hline \end{array}$$
☐

㉕
$$\begin{array}{r} 4 \\ + 1 \\ \hline \end{array}$$
☐

㉖
$$\begin{array}{r} 5 \\ - 4 \\ \hline \end{array}$$
☐

㉗
$$\begin{array}{r} 3 \\ - 2 \\ \hline \end{array}$$
☐

㉘
$$\begin{array}{r} 6 \\ + 0 \\ \hline \end{array}$$
☐

㉙
$$\begin{array}{r} 2 \\ - 0 \\ \hline \end{array}$$
☐

㉚
$$\begin{array}{r} 6 \\ - 4 \\ \hline \end{array}$$
☐

㉛
$$\begin{array}{r} 1 \\ + 1 \\ \hline \end{array}$$
☐

㉜
$$\begin{array}{r} 4 \\ - 0 \\ \hline \end{array}$$
☐

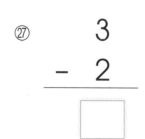

Find the sums or differences. Help the snake get back to the hole.

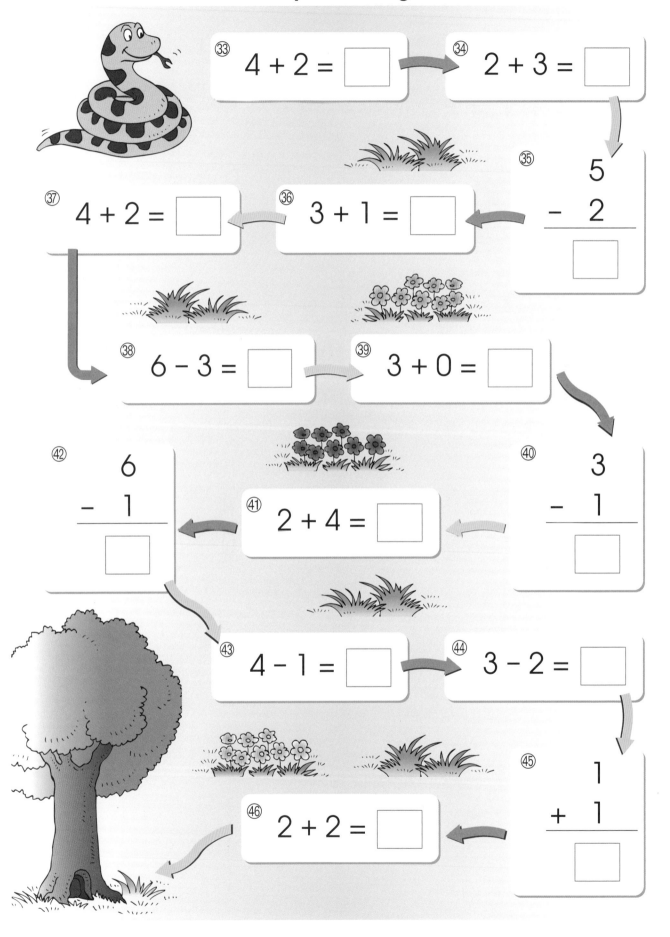

33 4 + 2 = ☐

34 2 + 3 = ☐

35 5 − 2 ☐

37 4 + 2 = ☐

36 3 + 1 = ☐

38 6 − 3 = ☐

39 3 + 0 = ☐

42 6 − 1 ☐

41 2 + 4 = ☐

40 3 − 1 ☐

43 4 − 1 = ☐

44 3 − 2 = ☐

45 1 + 1 ☐

46 2 + 2 = ☐

Complete.

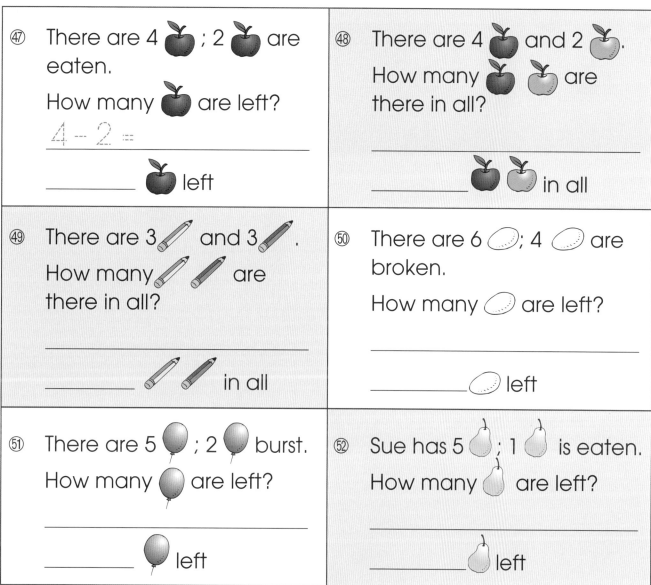

47. There are 4 🍎 ; 2 🍎 are eaten.
How many 🍎 are left?

4 – 2 = _____

_____ 🍎 left

48. There are 4 🍎 and 2 🍎.
How many 🍎 🍎 are there in all?

_____

_____ 🍎 🍎 in all

49. There are 3 ✏️ and 3 ✏️.
How many ✏️ ✏️ are there in all?

_____

_____ ✏️ ✏️ in all

50. There are 6 🥚 ; 4 🥚 are broken.
How many 🥚 are left?

_____

_____ 🥚 left

51. There are 5 🎈 ; 2 🎈 burst.
How many 🎈 are left?

_____

_____ 🎈 left

52. Sue has 5 🍐 ; 1 🍐 is eaten.
How many 🍐 are left?

_____

_____ 🍐 left

Just for Fun

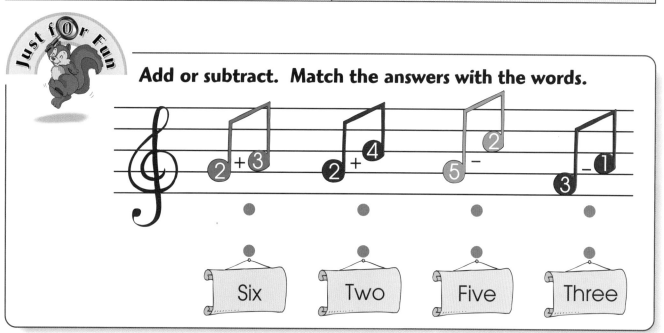

Add or subtract. Match the answers with the words.

2 + 3   2 + 4   5 – 2   3 – 1

Six   Two   Five   Three

Addition Facts to 10

HINTS:

- Adding 2 numbers:

  Count on from the bigger number.

  7 + 2 = ? ⟵ start from 7 and count 2 numbers more

  7 ⟶ 8 ⟶ 9   or

  Use a number line to find the sum.

  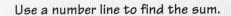

  6   7   8   9   10

  7 + 2 = 9

Complete each addition sentence.

①

   _6_ + _3_ = _____

②

   _____ + _____ = _____

③

   _____ + _____ = _____

④

   _____ + _____ = _____

⑤

   _____ + _____ = _____

⑥

   _____ + _____ = _____

⑦

   _____ + _____ = _____

Add.

⑧   5 + 4 = ☐   ⑨   7 + 3 = ☐

⑩   9 + 1 = ☐   ⑪   6 + 3 = ☐

⑫   7 + 2 = ☐   ⑬   8 + 2 = ☐

⑭   8 + 1 = ☐   ⑮   6 + 4 = ☐

⑯   6 + 2 = ☐   ⑰   5 + 3 = ☐

⑱   5 + 2 = ☐   ⑲   3 + 4 = ☐

⑳   10 + 0 = ☐   ㉑   4 + 4 = ☐

㉒	㉓	㉔	㉕
3 + 6 ☐	2 + 8 ☐	3 + 5 ☐	2 + 7 ☐

㉖	㉗	㉘	㉙
8 + 0 ☐	6 + 2 ☐	9 + 0 ☐	7 + 3 ☐

㉚	㉛	㉜	㉝
3 + 4 ☐	4 + 5 ☐	7 + 0 ☐	4 + 3 ☐

Complete the addition sentences for each number family. Draw the correct number of items.

㉞ 9    9 = _5_ + _4_

㉟ 9    9 = ____ + ____

㊱ 9    9 = ____ + ____

㊲ 9    9 = ____ + ____

㊳ 9    9 = ____ + ____

㊴ 8    8 = ____ + ____

㊵ 8    8 = ____ + ____

㊶ 8    8 = ____ + ____

㊷ 8    8 = ____ + ____

㊸ 8   8 = ____ + ____

㊹ 7    7 = ____ + ____

㊺ 7   7 = ____ + ____

㊻ 7    7 = ____ + ____

㊼ 7    7 = ____ + ____

Add.

(48)

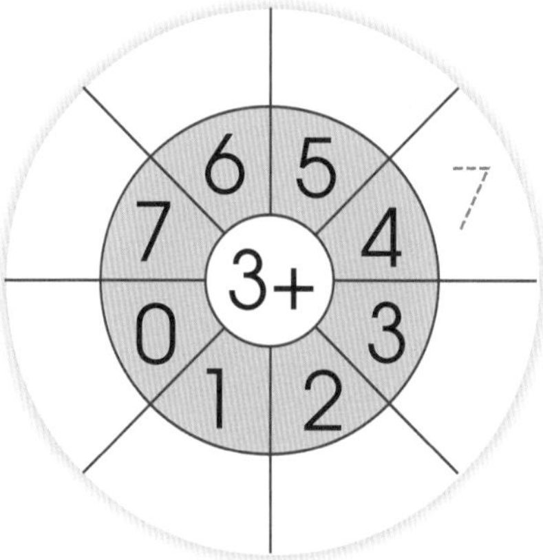

(49)

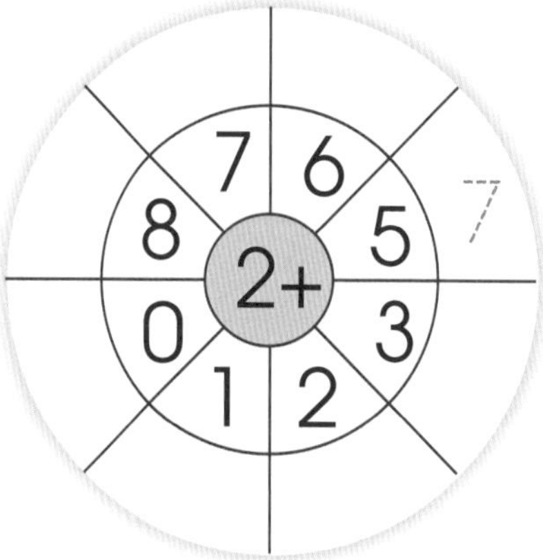

Complete.

(50) Sue has 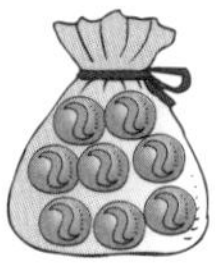 . Sam has 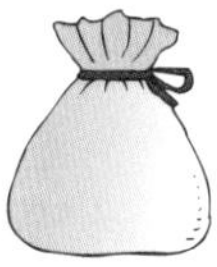 . How many 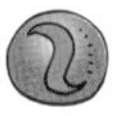 are there in all?

_______ + _______ = _______   _______ 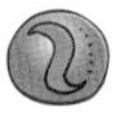 in all

(51) Jack has 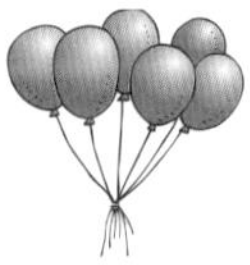 . Jane has 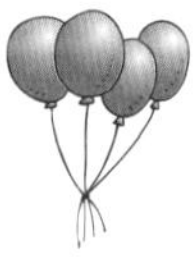 . How many 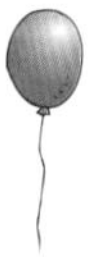 are there in all?

_______ + _______ = _______   _______ 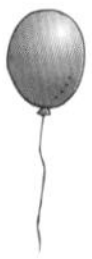 in all

(52) Bob has 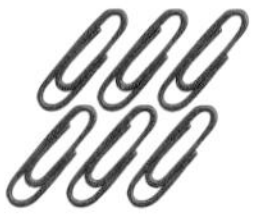 . Ben has 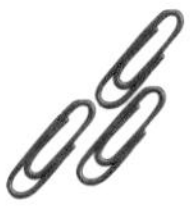 . How many 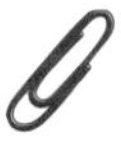 are there in all?

_______ + _______ = _______   _______ 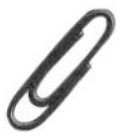 in all

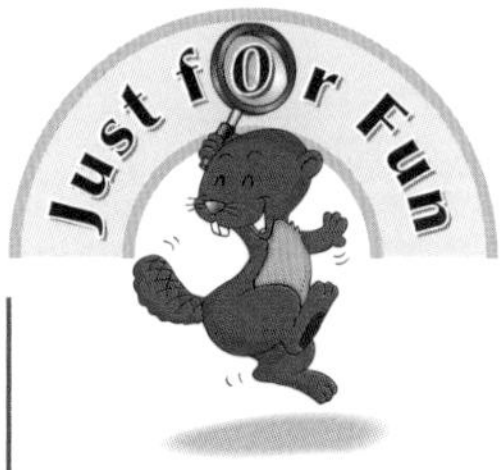

Fill in the missing numbers.

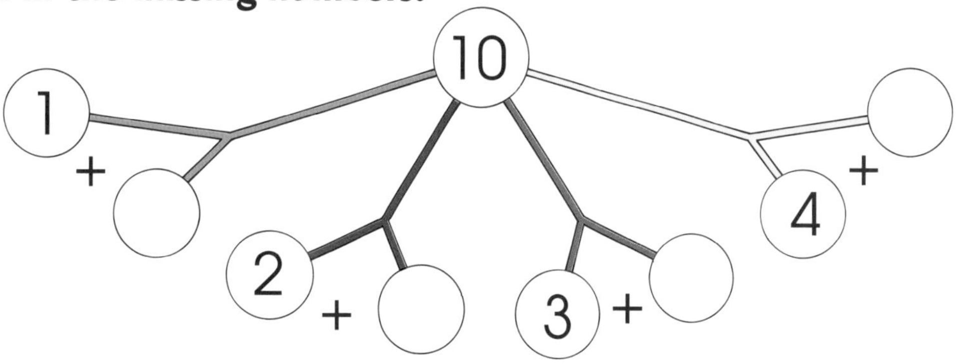

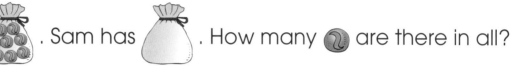

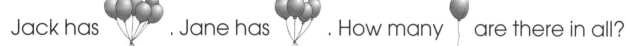

7 Subtraction Facts to 10

E X A M P L E S

1. 8 ; 2 were taken away ; 6 were left.

$$8 - 2 = 6$$

2. 9 ; 4 flew away ; 5 were left.

$$9 - 4 = 5$$

Complete each subtraction sentence.

HINTS:

- Subtracting 2 numbers:

  Count back from the bigger number.

  $9 - 3 = ?$ → start from 9 and count 3 numbers back

  $9 \rightarrow 8 \rightarrow 7 \rightarrow 6$ or

  Use a number line to find the difference.

  5   6   7   8   9   10

  $9 - 3 = 6$

①

    9 – 3 = _____

②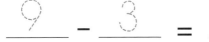

_____ – _____ = _____

③ 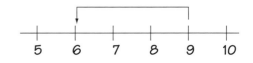 _____ – _____ = _____

④  _____ – _____ = _____

⑤  _____ – _____ = _____

⑥  _____ – _____ = _____

⑦  _____ – _____ = _____

Subtract.

⑧ 9 – 3 = ☐

⑨ 8 – 2 = ☐

⑩ 10 – 4 = ☐

⑪ 7 – 5 = ☐

⑫ 8 – 3 = ☐

⑬ 10 – 5 = ☐

⑭ 9 – 4 = ☐

⑮ 8 – 7 = ☐

⑯ 7 – 6 = ☐

⑰ 10 – 8 = ☐

⑱ 9 – 7 = ☐

⑲ 7 – 3 = ☐

⑳ 10 – 6 = ☐

㉑ 9 – 6 = ☐

㉒
```
   7
–  4
```
☐

㉓
```
  10
–  9
```
☐

㉔
```
   8
–  6
```
☐

㉕
```
   9
–  5
```
☐

㉖
```
   9
–  8
```
☐

㉗
```
   8
–  6
```
☐

㉘
```
  10
–  7
```
☐

㉙
```
   7
–  2
```
☐

㉚
```
  10
–  2
```
☐

㉛
```
   8
–  4
```
☐

㉜
```
  10
–  0
```
☐

㉝
```
   9
–  1
```
☐

73

Match and complete. Write the letters in ㊺ to solve the riddle.

㉞ $10 - 5 =$ 5 •

• $10 - 0 =$ ☐ Ⓖ

㉟ $8 - 4 =$ ☐ •

• $8 - 0 =$ ☐ Ⓒ

㊱ $10 - 2 =$ ☐ •

• $9 - 4 =$ ☐ Ⓢ

㊲ $10 - 0 =$ ☐ •

• $7 - 3 =$ ☐ Ⓘ

㊳ $7 - 6 =$ ☐ •

• $8 - 5 =$ ☐ Ⓝ

㊴ $8 - 8 =$ ☐ •

• $9 - 0 =$ ☐ Ⓐ

㊵ $9 - 6 =$ ☐ •

• $8 - 7 =$ ☐ Ⓞ

㊶ $10 - 1 =$ ☐ •

• $7 - 7 =$ ☐ Ⓦ

㊷ $7 - 5 =$ ☐ •

• $8 - 2 =$ ☐ Ⓗ

㊸ $6 - 0 =$ ☐ •

• $10 - 3 =$ ☐ Ⓣ

㊹ $9 - 2 =$ ☐ •

• $10 - 8 =$ ☐ Ⓓ

Riddle: Where is the White House?

㊺

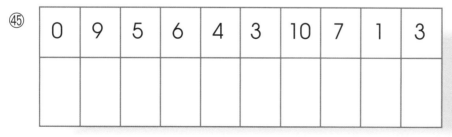

0	9	5	6	4	3	10	7	1	3		2		8

Subtract.

46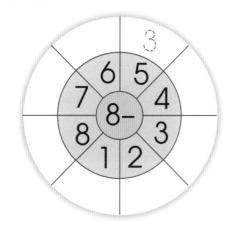

47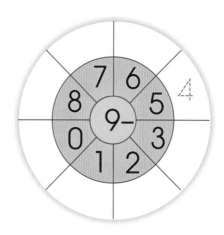

Complete.

48 Sue has . fly away. How many are left?

_____ – _____ = _____   _____ left

49 Jack has . are eaten. How many 🍒 are left?

_____ – _____ = _____   _____ 🍒 left

50 Mom has 🥚 . 🥚 are broken. How many 🥚 are left?

_____ – _____ = _____   _____ 🥚 left

Use – and = to make a subtraction sentence in each row. Circle each hidden subtraction sentence.

8	(10 – 2 = 8)		6
9	7	6	3	3
6	5	1	7	1
9	5	4	10	6

Addition and Subtraction Facts to 10

8

E X A M P L E

There are and and .

How many are there in all?

1 + 2 + 4 = 7

7 in all

method 1	method 2
1	1
+ 2	2
——	+ 4
3 → 3	——
+ 4	7
——	
7	

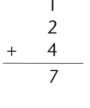

HINTS:

Adding 3 numbers:

Add the first 2 numbers. Write down the sum or bear it in mind. Then add the sum to the last number.

Complete each number sentence.

①

5 + 4

_____ = _____

②

_____ = _____

③

_____ = _____

④

_____ = _____

⑤

_____ = _____

⑥

_____ = _____

Add or subtract.

⑦ $2 + 2 + 3 =$ ☐ ⑧ $8 - 6 =$ ☐

⑨ $10 - 4 =$ ☐ ⑩ $6 + 4 =$ ☐

⑪ $7 + 2 =$ ☐ ⑫ $9 - 6 =$ ☐

⑬ $7 - 5 =$ ☐ ⑭ $1 + 0 + 6 =$ ☐

⑮ $8 + 2 =$ ☐ ⑯ $7 - 6 =$ ☐

⑰ $1 + 1 + 5 =$ ☐ ⑱ $9 - 2 =$ ☐

⑲ $6 + 3 =$ ☐ ⑳ $5 + 5 =$ ☐

㉑
$$\begin{array}{r} 8 \\ + 0 \\ \hline \end{array}$$
☐

㉒
$$\begin{array}{r} 4 \\ + 5 \\ \hline \end{array}$$
☐

㉓
$$\begin{array}{r} 2 \\ + 7 \\ \hline \end{array}$$
☐

㉔
$$\begin{array}{r} 4 \\ + 4 \\ \hline \end{array}$$
☐

㉕
$$\begin{array}{r} 9 \\ - 8 \\ \hline \end{array}$$
☐

㉖
$$\begin{array}{r} 10 \\ - 7 \\ \hline \end{array}$$
☐

㉗
$$\begin{array}{r} 7 \\ - 5 \\ \hline \end{array}$$
☐

㉘
$$\begin{array}{r} 8 \\ - 3 \\ \hline \end{array}$$
☐

㉙
$$\begin{array}{r} 2 \\ 0 \\ + 5 \\ \hline \end{array}$$
☐

㉚
$$\begin{array}{r} 3 \\ 1 \\ + 4 \\ \hline \end{array}$$
☐

㉛
$$\begin{array}{r} 5 \\ 2 \\ + 3 \\ \hline \end{array}$$
☐

㉜
$$\begin{array}{r} 6 \\ 1 \\ + 2 \\ \hline \end{array}$$
☐

Add or subtract. Help the cat find the path to the milk.

| 5 | + 3 | 8 | − 4 | ③③ | + 5 | ③④ |

| − 6 |

| ③⑤ |

| ③⑨ | + 8 | ③⑧ | − 3 | ③⑦ | − 5 | ③⑥ | + 7 |

| − 0 |

| ④⓪ |

| − 4 | ④① | − 2 | ④② | + 5 | ④③ | − 3 |

| ④④ |

| + 2 |

| − 1 | ④⑦ | + 0 | ④⑥ | − 3 | ④⑤ |

| ④⑧ |

| + 6 |

| ④⑨ | − 7 | ⑤⓪ | + 4 | ⑤① |

Complete.

52 8 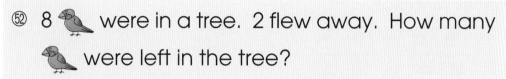 were in a tree. 2 flew away. How many were left in the tree?

_____ left

53 6 turtles were on a rock. 4 more came. How many turtles were on the rock?

_____ were on the rock

54 Sam has 5 shells. Sue has 4 shells. How many do they have altogether?

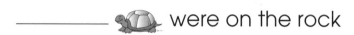

_____ altogether

55 9 monkeys were in a tree. 6 jumped down. How many monkeys were left in the tree?

_____ left

56 Sue has 2 lollipops. Sam has 4 lollipops. Ann has 1 lollipop. How many do they have altogether?

_____ altogether

Pick out any two balls each time.

The smallest sum is _____.

The largest difference is _____.

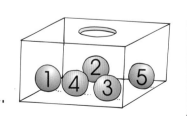

79

Complete each number sentence.

①

_____ = _____

②

_____ = _____

③

_____ = _____

Find the sums or differences.

④ $10 - 5 = \boxed{}$ ⑤ $4 + 2 = \boxed{}$

⑥ $9 - 7 = \boxed{}$ ⑦ $8 - 6 = \boxed{}$

⑧ $2 + 5 = \boxed{}$ ⑨ $6 - 5 = \boxed{}$

⑩ $3 + 3 = \boxed{}$ ⑪ $7 + 0 = \boxed{}$

⑫ $6 + 0 + 3 = \boxed{}$ ⑬ $4 + 1 + 2 = \boxed{}$

⑭
$$\begin{array}{r} 0 \\ +\ 9 \\ \hline \end{array}$$

⑮
$$\begin{array}{r} 5 \\ -\ 4 \\ \hline \end{array}$$

⑯
$$\begin{array}{r} 10 \\ -\ 7 \\ \hline \end{array}$$

⑰
$$\begin{array}{r} 3 \\ +\ 5 \\ \hline \end{array}$$

⑱
$$\begin{array}{r} 6 \\ -\ 4 \\ \hline \end{array}$$

⑲
$$\begin{array}{r} 3 \\ +\ 4 \\ \hline \end{array}$$

⑳
$$\begin{array}{r} 8 \\ -\ 4 \\ \hline \end{array}$$

㉑
$$\begin{array}{r} 1 \\ +\ 7 \\ \hline \end{array}$$

In each group, color the pieces that match the number.

㉒  5 + 3   10 − 2   3 + 6   9 − 1

㉓  4 + 1   9 − 3   8 − 2   3 + 3

㉔  1 + 8   10 − 2   5 + 4   9 − 0

㉕

10 − 5   3 + 2   8 − 2   4 + 1

㉖  4 + 3   9 − 2   10 − 3   2 + 6

Complete the tables. Write + or − in the ◯ .

㉗

+ 3	
2	5
7	
5	

㉘

− 4	
8	
4	
6	

㉙

◯	2
9	7
5	3
6	4

㉚

◯	4
2	6
6	10
5	9

Write the numbers.

③ $10 - \boxed{}$

③ $9 - \boxed{}$

③ $8 - \boxed{}$

③ $7 - \boxed{}$

5

③ $3 + \boxed{}$

③ $2 + \boxed{}$

③ $1 + \boxed{}$

③ $0 + \boxed{}$

Put + or – in each box.

③
$$\boxed{} \begin{array}{r} 10 \\ 2 \\ \hline 8 \end{array}$$

④
$$\boxed{} \begin{array}{r} 2 \\ 7 \\ \hline 9 \end{array}$$

④
$$\boxed{} \begin{array}{r} 5 \\ 4 \\ \hline 9 \end{array}$$

④
$$\boxed{} \begin{array}{r} 8 \\ 6 \\ \hline 2 \end{array}$$

④
$$\boxed{} \begin{array}{r} 7 \\ 5 \\ \hline 2 \end{array}$$

④
$$\boxed{} \begin{array}{r} 3 \\ 4 \\ \hline 7 \end{array}$$

④
$$\boxed{} \begin{array}{r} 9 \\ 3 \\ \hline 6 \end{array}$$

④
$$\boxed{} \begin{array}{r} 1 \\ 5 \\ \hline 6 \end{array}$$

④
$$\boxed{} \begin{array}{r} 8 \\ 4 \\ \hline 4 \end{array}$$

④
$$\boxed{} \begin{array}{r} 9 \\ 1 \\ \hline 8 \end{array}$$

④
$$\boxed{} \begin{array}{r} 4 \\ 2 \\ \hline 6 \end{array}$$

⑤
$$\boxed{} \begin{array}{r} 3 \\ 6 \\ \hline 9 \end{array}$$

Fill in the numbers.

⑤ $6 + \boxed{} = 7$

⑤ $1 + \boxed{} = 4$

⑤ $6 - \boxed{} = 2$

⑤ $7 - \boxed{} = 3$

⑤ $4 + \boxed{} = 8$

⑤ $2 + \boxed{} = 5$

Complete.

⑤⑦ 10 🐦 are in the sky. 2 🐦 land on the grass. How many 🐦 are left in the sky? _____ 🐦 left	
⑤⑧ 6 🐸 are in a pond. 3 🐸 jump away. How many 🐸 are left in the pond? _____ 🐸 left	
⑤⑨ 5 🪰 are in the sky. 4 🪰 are on the water. How many 🪰 are there in all? _____ 🪰 in all	
⑥⓪ There are 2 🌹 and 6 🌹. How many 🌹🌹 are there in all? _____ 🌹🌹 in all	
⑥① 4 🐒 are in the tree. 3 🐒 are on the grass. How many 🐒 are there in all? _____ 🐒 in all	
⑥② 8 🍌 are in the tree. The 🐒 eats 4 🍌. How many 🍌 are left in the tree? _____ 🍌 left	

83

9 Addition Facts to 15

$$8 + 7 = 15$$

HINTS:

- Counting on helps you find the sum faster.

- Different addition sentences may give the same SUM.

Draw the lines. Complete the addition sentences.

①

$$6 + \underline{9} = 15$$

②

$$6 + \underline{} = 13$$

③

$$\underline{} + 4 = 12$$

④

$$10 + \underline{} = \underline{}$$

⑤

$$\underline{} + 1 = \underline{}$$

⑥

$$\underline{} + 9 = \underline{}$$

Add.

⑦ 12 + 3 = ☐   ⑧ 11 + 2 = ☐

⑨ 10 + 4 = ☐   ⑩ 9 + 6 = ☐

⑪ 8 + 6 = ☐   ⑫ 7 + 5 = ☐

⑬ 9 + 3 = ☐   ⑭ 6 + 7 = ☐

⑮ 14 + 0 = ☐   ⑯ 2 + 9 = ☐

⑰ 3 + 8 = ☐   ⑱ 5 + 6 = ☐

⑲ 7 + 7 = ☐   ⑳ 13 + 2 = ☐

㉑
$$\begin{array}{r} 4 \\ +\ 9 \\ \hline \end{array}$$

㉒
$$\begin{array}{r} 11 \\ +\ 4 \\ \hline \end{array}$$

㉓
$$\begin{array}{r} 6 \\ +\ 6 \\ \hline \end{array}$$

㉔
$$\begin{array}{r} 7 \\ +\ 4 \\ \hline \end{array}$$

㉕
$$\begin{array}{r} 8 \\ +\ 4 \\ \hline \end{array}$$

㉖
$$\begin{array}{r} 9 \\ +\ 5 \\ \hline \end{array}$$

㉗
$$\begin{array}{r} 5 \\ +\ 8 \\ \hline \end{array}$$

㉘
$$\begin{array}{r} 11 \\ +\ 3 \\ \hline \end{array}$$

㉙
$$\begin{array}{r} 14 \\ +\ 1 \\ \hline \end{array}$$

㉚
$$\begin{array}{r} 7 \\ +\ 8 \\ \hline \end{array}$$

㉛
$$\begin{array}{r} 9 \\ +\ 6 \\ \hline \end{array}$$

㉜
$$\begin{array}{r} 12 \\ +\ 2 \\ \hline \end{array}$$

Fill in the missing numbers.

㉝ 3 + ☐

㉟ 4 + ☐

㊲ 5 + ☐

㊴ 6 + ☐

㊶ 7 + ☐

14

㉞ 8 + ☐

㊱ 9 + ☐

㊳ 10 + ☐

㊵ 11 + ☐

㊷ 12 + ☐

Complete. Color the balloon with the largest sum in each group.

㊸

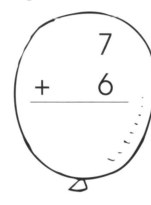

| 5
+ 6 | 8
+ 4 | 7
+ 6 | 9
+ 6 |

㊹

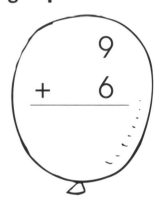

| 11
+ 2 | 10
+ 4 | 2
+ 9 | 5
+ 7 |

㊺ (3 + 8 = ____)   (6 + 6 = ____)   (11 + 3 = ____)

㊻ (12 + 3 = ____)   (6 + 8 = ____)   (9 + 3 = ____)

Complete.

㊼ There are 8 and 6 . How many  are there in all? _____  in all.		
㊽ 10 are on the plate. 3 are in the bag. How many  are there in all? _____  in all		
㊾ 12  are in the basket. 0  are on the table. How many  are there in all? _____  in all		
㊿ 4 are in Sam's left hand. 7 are in his right hand. How many does Sam have in all? _____ in all		

Complete.

$$9 + 6 = 10 + \boxed{}$$

$$2 + 5 = 8 - \boxed{}$$

10 Subtraction Facts to 15

$15 - 4 = 11$

HINTS:

- Counting back helps you find the difference faster.

- Different subtraction sentences may give the same DIFFERENCE.

Follow the example to complete each subtraction sentence.

①

14 – 6 = _____

②

_____ – 7 = _____

③

_____ – 8 = _____

④

_____ – 10 = _____

⑤

_____ – 9 = _____

⑥

_____ – 11 = _____

88

Subtract.

⑦ 13 − 4 = ☐   ⑧ 12 − 6 = ☐

⑨ 15 − 7 = ☐   ⑩ 14 − 9 = ☐

⑪ 11 − 6 = ☐   ⑫ 13 − 8 = ☐

⑬ 12 − 8 = ☐   ⑭ 15 − 9 = ☐

⑮ 14 − 4 = ☐   ⑯ 13 − 0 = ☐

⑰ 13 − 2 = ☐   ⑱ 11 − 3 = ☐

⑲ 15 − 13 = ☐   ⑳ 12 − 3 = ☐

㉑
```
  11
-  7
─────
☐
```

㉒
```
  13
-  1
─────
☐
```

㉓
```
  15
-  5
─────
☐
```

㉔
```
  12
- 12
─────
☐
```

㉕
```
  14
- 10
─────
☐
```

㉖
```
  15
-  9
─────
☐
```

㉗
```
  12
-  4
─────
☐
```

㉘
```
  11
-  4
─────
☐
```

㉙
```
  13
-  9
─────
☐
```

㉚
```
  14
- 12
─────
☐
```

㉛
```
  11
-  5
─────
☐
```

㉜
```
  12
-  7
─────
☐
```

Subtract. Help Baby Bear find Mother Bear.

㉝ 14 − 7 =

㉞ 13 − 5 =

㊲ 11 − 2 =

㉟
$$12 \\ -5$$

㊳
$$13 \\ -11$$

㊱ 15 − 6 =

㊴ 14 − 8 =

㊵ 12 − 2 =

㊷
$$11 \\ -8$$

㊶ 13 − 3 =

㊸ 14 − 5 =

Complete.

㊹ There are 14  are eaten.
How many  are left?

_____  left

$$\begin{array}{r} 14 \\ -\ 8 \\ \hline \end{array}$$

㊺ Sue has 12 . Sam has 7 .
How many more  does Sue have than Sam?

_____ more

㊻ There are 13  on the plate and 5  in the bag.
How many more  are there on the plate?

_____ more

㊼ There are 15 . 6  burst.
How many  are left?

_____  left

Just for Fun

Count on to find the path for the monkey.
Color the path.

12	18	16	17	15
14	16	15	18	17
15	13	14	19	20
11	12	17	18	16
17	13	12	11	12

11 Addition and Subtraction Facts to 15

There are 12 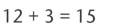 and 3  .

1. How many  are there in all?

   12 + 3 = 15   15  in all

2. How many more are there than  ?

   12 – 3 = 9   9 more

HINTS:

- Vertical addition:

  $$\begin{array}{r} 1\,2 \\ +\ \ 3 \\ \hline 1\,5 \end{array}$$ ⟵ align on the right-hand side

- Vertical subtraction:

  $$\begin{array}{r} 1\,2 \\ -\ \ 3 \\ \hline 9 \end{array}$$ ⟵ align on the right-hand side

Add or cross out the correct number of items. Complete each number sentence.

①

$\underline{15} - 6 = \underline{\hspace{2cm}}$

②

$9 + \underline{5} = 14$

③

$7 + \underline{\hspace{1.5cm}} = 15$

④

$\underline{\hspace{1.5cm}} - 5 = \underline{\hspace{2cm}}$

⑤

$\underline{\hspace{1.5cm}} - 8 = \underline{\hspace{2cm}}$

⑥

$9 + \underline{\hspace{1.5cm}} = 13$

92

Add or subtract.

⑦ 13 − 7 = [ ]   ⑧ 8 + 5 = [ ]

⑨ 6 + 8 = [ ]   ⑩ 11 − 7 = [ ]

⑪ 5 + 10 = [ ]   ⑫ 12 − 6 = [ ]

⑬ 14 − 6 = [ ]   ⑭ 8 + 3 = [ ]

⑮ 15 − 9 = [ ]   ⑯ 7 + 7 = [ ]

⑰ 11 − 10 = [ ]   ⑱ 15 + 0 = [ ]

⑲ 12 + 3 = [ ]   ⑳ 15 − 6 = [ ]

㉑
```
    4
+   9
------
[     ]
```

㉒
```
   14
−   9
------
[     ]
```

㉓
```
   11
+   2
------
[     ]
```

㉔
```
   12
−  10
------
[     ]
```

㉕
```
    9
−   6
------
[     ]
```

㉖
```
   12
−   5
------
[     ]
```

㉗
```
   13
−  11
------
[     ]
```

㉘
```
   13
+   2
------
[     ]
```

㉙
```
   15
−  12
------
[     ]
```

㉚
```
    6
+   8
------
[     ]
```

㉛
```
    7
+   5
------
[     ]
```

㉜
```
   14
−   8
------
[     ]
```

93

Complete the tables.

㉝

+	4	5	6
7			
8			
9			15

㉞

13	14	15	−
			7
			8
		6	9

Match.

㉟

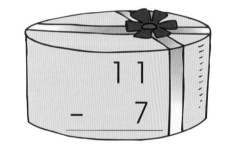

$$15 - 11$$

$$14 - 9$$

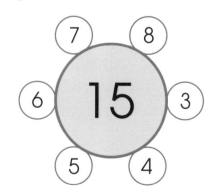

$$14 - 11$$

In each group, color the two numbers that give the sum in the center.

㊱

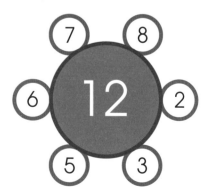

㊲

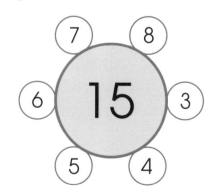

Complete.

㊳ Jack has 6 🍭. Jane has 8 🍭. How many 🍭 do they have altogether? _____ 🍭 altogether	6 + 8 ————
㊴ Sam has 13 🍭. Sue has 9 🍭. How many more 🍭 does Sam have than Sue? _____ more 🍭	
㊵ There are 14 🐚 and 10 🐚. How many more 🐚 are there than 🐚 ? _____ more 🐚	
㊶ There are 5 🐰 and 6 🐰. How many 🐰 🐰 are there in all? _____ 🐰 🐰 in all	

Color the path for Little Ant to get the food. Start from 0. Count by 5's to 50.

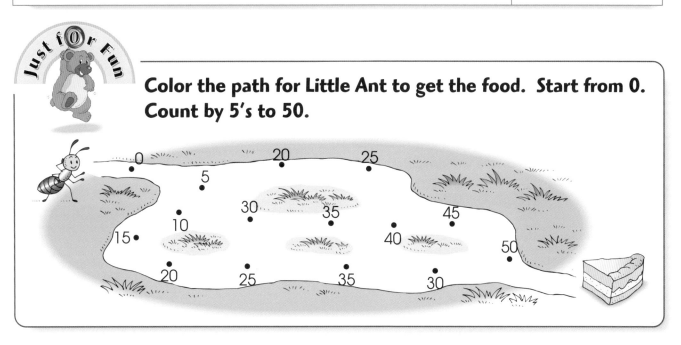

 **Addition Facts to 20**

EXAMPLE

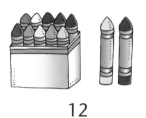

12   +   8   =   20

HINTS:

Adding means joining two groups or putting two groups together.

Complete each addition sentence.

①

____ + ____ = _____

②

____ + ____ = _____

③

____ + ____ = _____

④

____ + ____ = _____

⑤

____ + ____ = _____

⑥

____ + ____ = _____

Add.

⑦ $16 + 4 =$ ☐ ⑧ $13 + 6 =$ ☐

⑨ $11 + 8 =$ ☐ ⑩ $15 + 4 =$ ☐

⑪ $12 + 7 =$ ☐ ⑫ $17 + 3 =$ ☐

⑬ $10 + 9 =$ ☐ ⑭ $14 + 4 =$ ☐

⑮ $8 + 9 =$ ☐ ⑯ $19 + 1 =$ ☐

⑰ $15 + 2 =$ ☐ ⑱ $12 + 5 =$ ☐

⑲ $13 + 4 =$ ☐ ⑳ $11 + 9 =$ ☐

㉑
$$\begin{array}{r} 17 \\ + \ \ 2 \\ \hline \end{array}$$
☐

㉒
$$\begin{array}{r} 10 \\ + \ \ 8 \\ \hline \end{array}$$
☐

㉓
$$\begin{array}{r} 15 \\ + \ \ 5 \\ \hline \end{array}$$
☐

㉔
$$\begin{array}{r} 12 \\ + \ \ 6 \\ \hline \end{array}$$
☐

㉕
$$\begin{array}{r} 11 \\ + \ \ 5 \\ \hline \end{array}$$
☐

㉖
$$\begin{array}{r} 13 \\ + \ \ 6 \\ \hline \end{array}$$
☐

㉗
$$\begin{array}{r} 14 \\ + \ \ 3 \\ \hline \end{array}$$
☐

㉘
$$\begin{array}{r} 16 \\ + \ \ 3 \\ \hline \end{array}$$
☐

㉙
$$\begin{array}{r} 18 \\ + \ \ 2 \\ \hline \end{array}$$
☐

㉚
$$\begin{array}{r} 9 \\ + \ \ 7 \\ \hline \end{array}$$
☐

㉛
$$\begin{array}{r} 19 \\ + \ \ 1 \\ \hline \end{array}$$
☐

㉜
$$\begin{array}{r} 10 \\ + \ 10 \\ \hline \end{array}$$
☐

Match and complete. Write the letters in ㊸ to solve the riddle.

㉝ 15 + 3 = _____ •   • Ⓝ 13 + 3 = _____

㉞ 10 + 6 = _____ •   • Ⓚ 12 + 2 = _____

㉟ 9 + 5 = _____ •   • Ⓡ 16 + 2 = _____

㊱ 11 + 6 = _____ •   • Ⓗ 16 + 4 = _____

㊲ 12 + 8 = _____ •   • Ⓒ 16 + 1 = _____

㊳ 13 + 2 = _____ •   • Ⓔ 15 + 4 = _____

㊴ 16 + 3 = _____ •   • Ⓓ 14 + 1 = _____

㊵ 11 + 1 = _____ •   • Ⓐ 6 + 5 = _____

㊶ 9 + 4 = _____ •   • Ⓕ 10 + 2 = _____

㊷ 7 + 4 = _____ •   • Ⓘ 6 + 7 = _____

Riddle: What do you need when you sweat?

㊸

20	11	16	15	14	19	18	17	20	13	19	12
A	h										

Complete.

44   There are 10 🎂 and 10 🍰 in the bakery.
How many 🎂 🍰 are there in all?

_____ = _____   _____ 🎂 🍰 in all

45   There are 12 🥧 and 6 🥟 .
How many 🥧 🥟 are there in all?

_____ = _____   _____ 🥧 🥟 in all

46   There are 8 🫐 and 8 🧁 .
How many 🫐 🧁 are there in all?

_____ = _____   _____ 🫐 🧁 in all

47   There are 9 🥖 . The baker makes 10 more 🥖 .
How many 🥖 are there in all?

_____ = _____   _____ 🥖 in all

48   There are 13 🥯 on 🍽 and 4 🥯 in 📦 .
How many 🥯 are there in all?

_____ = _____   _____ 🥯 in all

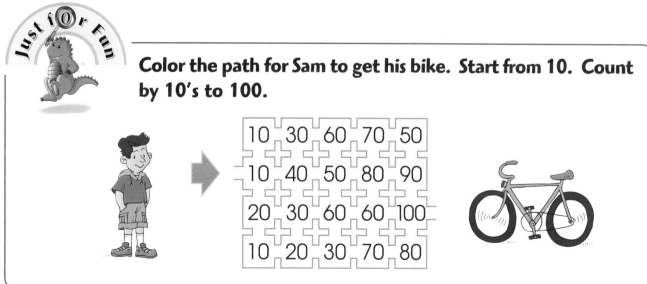

Just for Fun

Color the path for Sam to get his bike. Start from 10. Count by 10's to 100.

10	30	60	70	50
10	40	50	80	90
20	30	60	60	100
10	20	30	70	80

13 Subtraction Facts to 20

EXAMPLE

17   –   5   =   12

INTS:

Subtracting means taking one group away from another.

Complete each subtraction sentence.

①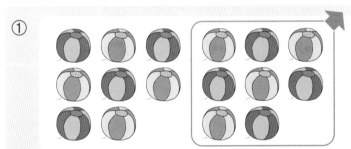

$$16 - 8 = \underline{\hspace{2cm}}$$

②

$$\underline{\hspace{1.5cm}} - \underline{\hspace{1cm}} = \underline{\hspace{2cm}}$$

③

$$\underline{\hspace{1.5cm}} - \underline{\hspace{1cm}} = \underline{\hspace{2cm}}$$

④

$$\underline{\hspace{1.5cm}} - \underline{\hspace{1cm}} = \underline{\hspace{2cm}}$$

⑤

$$\underline{\hspace{1.5cm}} - \underline{\hspace{1cm}} = \underline{\hspace{2cm}}$$

⑥

$$\underline{\hspace{1.5cm}} - \underline{\hspace{1cm}} = \underline{\hspace{2cm}}$$

Add or subtract.

⑦ 18 − 7 = ⬜   ⑧ 16 − 9 = ⬜

⑨ 20 − 11 = ⬜   ⑩ 19 − 4 = ⬜

⑪ 17 − 8 = ⬜   ⑫ 18 − 12 = ⬜

⑬ 16 − 4 = ⬜   ⑭ 20 − 6 = ⬜

⑮ 19 − 17 = ⬜   ⑯ 17 − 4 = ⬜

⑰ 20 − 2 = ⬜   ⑱ 16 − 13 = ⬜

⑲ 18 − 4 = ⬜   ⑳ 17 − 11 = ⬜

㉑
```
   19
 −  3
 ____
 ⬜
```

㉒
```
   16
 − 10
 ____
 ⬜
```

㉓
```
   18
 −  8
 ____
 ⬜
```

㉔
```
   17
 −  5
 ____
 ⬜
```

㉕
```
   20
 −  5
 ____
 ⬜
```

㉖
```
   17
 −  8
 ____
 ⬜
```

㉗
```
   16
 −  9
 ____
 ⬜
```

㉘
```
   19
 − 13
 ____
 ⬜
```

㉙
```
   18
 − 15
 ____
 ⬜
```

㉚
```
   16
 − 12
 ____
 ⬜
```

㉛
```
   19
 −  5
 ____
 ⬜
```

㉜
```
   20
 −  7
 ____
 ⬜
```

Subtract. Help Little Bunny go through the forest.

㉝ 16 – 10 = ☐

㉞ 20 – 13 = ☐

㉟
$$\begin{array}{r} 18 \\ -7 \\ \hline \end{array}$$
☐

㊱ 17 – 12 = ☐

㊲ 16 – 11 = ☐

㊳
$$\begin{array}{r} 16 \\ -15 \\ \hline \end{array}$$
☐

㊴ 18 – 16 = ☐

㊵ 19 – 14 = ☐

㊶
$$\begin{array}{r} 17 \\ -15 \\ \hline \end{array}$$
☐

㊷ 18 – 11 = ☐

㊸
$$\begin{array}{r} 19 \\ -10 \\ \hline \end{array}$$
☐

㊹ 18 – 6 = ☐

Complete.

㊺ Sue bought 18 ✏ . Sam bought 12 ✏ .

How many more ✏ did Sue buy than Sam?

_____ = _____   _____ more ✏

㊻ Jack has 17 🗒 . Jane has 9 🗒 .

How many more 🗒 does Jack have than Jane?

_____ = _____   _____ more 🗒

㊼ Bob has 20 🧱 . Ben has 18 🧱 .

How many more 🧱 does Bob have than Ben?

_____ = _____   _____ more 🧱

㊽ There are 16 ⚾ on the table. 5 ⚾ roll off.

How many ⚾ are left on the table?

_____ = _____   _____ ⚾ left

㊾ There are 19 children in the playground. 9 of them are boys.

How many girls are there in the playground?

_____ = _____   _____ girls

Just for Fun

Color the cards with the same answers.

| 18 – 4 | 12 – 8 | 16 – 11 |

| 19 – 5 | 17 – 4 | 20 – 6 | 14 – 10 |

103

14 Addition and Subtraction Facts to 20

EXAMPLES

Sue has 18 ✏. Sam has 2 ✏.

1. How many ✏ do they have altogether?

   18 + 2 = 20   20 ✏ altogether

2. How many more ✏ does Sue have than Sam?

   18 − 2 = 16   16 more ✏

HINTS:

Read each question carefully to see if it is an addition or a subtraction problem.

Draw a line to show 2 groups or circle the group to be taken away. Complete each number sentence.

①

16 + _4_ = 20

②

18 − 6 = _12_

③

12 + ___ = _____

④

_____ − 5 = _____

⑤

_____ − 14 = _____

⑥

8 + ___ = _____

Add or subtract.

⑦ 18 – 4 =

⑧ 16 + 3 =

⑨ 15 + 4 =

⑩ 19 – 12 =

⑪ 12 – 9 =

⑫ 20 – 8 =

⑬ 17 – 14 =

⑭ 17 + 2 =

⑮ 16 – 12 =

⑯ 15 + 5 =

⑰ 19 + 1 =

⑱ 18 – 11 =

⑲ 20 + 0 =

⑳ 17 – 9 =

㉑
```
   15
+   2
───────
```

㉒
```
   16
–   9
───────
```

㉓
```
   17
+   3
───────
```

㉔
```
   20
–   9
───────
```

㉕
```
   18
– 15
───────
```

㉖
```
   16
+   4
───────
```

㉗
```
   17
– 13
───────
```

㉘
```
   19
–   9
───────
```

㉙
```
   20
–   4
───────
```

㉚
```
   17
–   5
───────
```

㉛
```
   18
+   2
───────
```

㉜
```
   15
+   3
───────
```

In each group, color the plates that match the number.

 ㉝ 19

| 12 + 7 | 20 − 1 | 14 + 4 | 13 + 6 |

 ㉞ 16

| 20 − 4 | 12 + 3 | 19 − 3 | 9 + 7 |

 ㉟ 13

| 9 + 5 | 19 − 6 | 17 − 4 | 7 + 6 |

 ㊱ 15

| 18 − 3 | 9 + 7 | 17 − 2 | 11 + 4 |

 ㊲ 18

| 18 − 0 | 20 − 2 | 10 + 8 | 12 + 5 |

 ㊳ 11

| 16 − 4 | 7 + 4 | 17 − 6 | 9 + 2 |

 ㊴ 12

| 8 + 4 | 19 − 7 | 6 + 5 | 16 − 4 |

Complete.

㊵ There are 17 🌹 and 12 🌷. How many more 🌹 are there than 🌷? _____ more 🌹	 17 12
㊶ Mom bought 18 🍦. 8 🍦 melted. How many 🍦 were left? _____ 🍦 left	
㊷ Uncle Tom has 20 🎈. 6 🎈 burst. How many 🎈 are left? _____ 🎈 left	
㊸ Bob has 13 🏷. He buys 6 more 🏷. How many 🏷 does Bob have now? _____ 🏷	
㊹ Jack has 16 🍭. He has 3 🍭 more than Jane. How many 🍭 does Jane have? _____ 🍭	

Just for Fun

Put the numbers in the correct counting order, starting with the largest number.

 12   48   65   7   32   56   29

_____ _____ _____ _____ _____ _____ _____

E X A M P L E S

1.

goes up by one

goes up by one

(
6 + 6 = 12

7 + 6 = 13

8 + 6 = 14
)

goes up by one

goes up by one

2.

goes up by one

goes up by one

(
12 – 7 = 5

13 – 7 = 6

14 – 7 = 7
)

goes up by one

goes up by one

HINTS:

- Knowing the addition or subtraction patterns may help you find the sum or difference faster.

- Using tens may also help you find the sum and difference faster.

    e.g. $7 + 5 = 7 + 3 + 2$
    $= 10 + 2$
    $= 12$

    $12 - 4 = 10 + 2 - 4$
    $= 10 - 4 + 2$
    $= 6 + 2$
    $= 8$

Complete the number sentences.

① $7 + 7 = 14$

   a. $8 + 7 = \underline{\hspace{1.5cm}}$

   b. $9 + 7 = \underline{\hspace{1.5cm}}$

   c. $10 + 7 = \underline{\hspace{1.5cm}}$

   d. $11 + 7 = \underline{\hspace{1.5cm}}$

   e. $12 + 7 = \underline{\hspace{1.5cm}}$

② $8 + 8 = 16$

   a. $8 + 9 = \underline{\hspace{1.5cm}}$

   b. $8 + 10 = \underline{\hspace{1.5cm}}$

   c. $8 + 11 = \underline{\hspace{1.5cm}}$

   d. $8 + 12 = \underline{\hspace{1.5cm}}$

③ $5 + 5 = 10$

   a. $5 + 6 = \underline{\hspace{1.5cm}}$

   b. $5 + 7 = \underline{\hspace{1.5cm}}$

   c. $5 + 8 = \underline{\hspace{1.5cm}}$

   d. $5 + 9 = \underline{\hspace{1.5cm}}$

④   18 − 8 = 10

   a.   18 − 9 = _____

   b.   18 − 10 = _____

   c.   18 − 11 = _____

   d.   18 − 12 = _____

   e.   18 − 13 = _____

⑤   12 − 6 = 6

   a.   13 − 6 = _____

   b.   14 − 6 = _____

   c.   15 − 6 = _____

   d.   16 − 6 = _____

   e.   17 − 6 = _____

Draw and complete.

⑥ 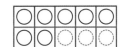   7 + 5

       = 10 + _2___

   = _____

⑦    8 + 7

       = 10 + _____

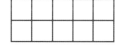   = _____

⑧    9 + 4

       = 10 + _____

   = _____

⑨ 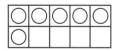   6 + 8

       = 10 + _____

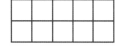   = _____

⑩ 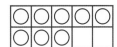   8 + 9

       = 10 + _____

    = _____

⑪     9 + 6

       = 10 + _____

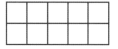   = _____

Cross out the correct number of items and complete the subtraction sentences.

⑫
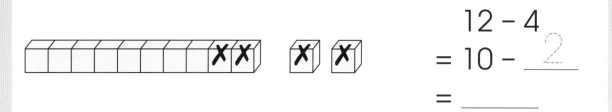

$12 - 4$

$= 10 - \underline{}$

$= \underline{}$

⑬
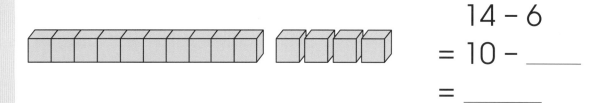

$14 - 6$

$= 10 - \underline{}$

$= \underline{}$

⑭
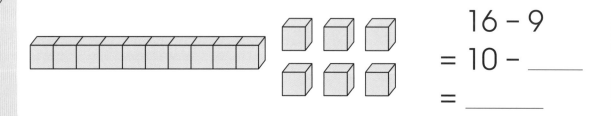

$16 - 9$

$= 10 - \underline{}$

$= \underline{}$

⑮
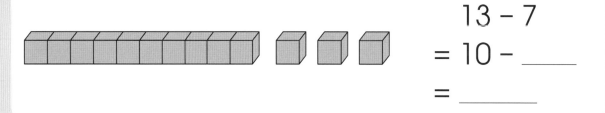

$13 - 7$

$= 10 - \underline{}$

$= \underline{}$

⑯
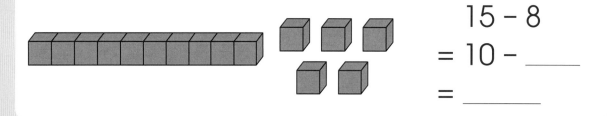

$15 - 8$

$= 10 - \underline{}$

$= \underline{}$

⑰

$17 - 9$

$= 10 - \underline{}$

$= \underline{}$

Add.

⑱
```
    2
    4
+   8
```
☐

⑲
```
    3
    2
+   7
```
☐

⑳
```
    7
    2
+   9
```
☐

㉑
```
    8
    0
+   7
```
☐

㉒
```
    9
    1
+   6
```
☐

㉓
```
    5
    5
+   7
```
☐

㉔
```
    2
    8
+   9
```
☐

㉕
```
    3
    7
+   5
```
☐

Complete. Color the party hats red if the answers are odd numbers. Color the hats yellow if the answers are even numbers.

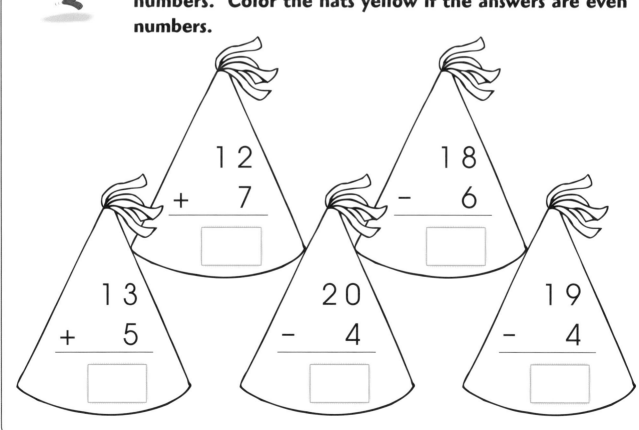

```
  12
+  7
```
☐

```
  18
-  6
```
☐

```
  13
+  5
```
☐

```
  20
-  4
```
☐

```
  19
-  4
```
☐

Addition and Subtraction with Money

How many cents are there in the piggy bank?

$$5 + 1 + 1$$
$$= 7$$

There are 7¢ in the piggy bank.

How many cents are there in each set?

① 4¢

②

③

④

The children go to a garage sale. Circle the coins needed to buy each item.

⑤ 4 ¢

⑥ 8 ¢

⑦ 10 ¢

⑧ 5 ¢

How much change do they get?

⑨  $\underline{10}$ ¢ – $\underline{8}$ ¢ = _____ ¢

⑩  _____ ¢ – _____ ¢ = _____ ¢

⑪  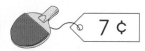 _____ ¢ – _____ ¢ = _____ ¢

⑫  _____ ¢ – _____ ¢ = _____ ¢

⑬  _____ ¢ – _____ ¢ = _____ ¢

How much more do they need?

⑭ $\underline{8}$ ¢ – $\underline{5}$ ¢ = _____ ¢

⑮  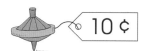 _____ ¢ – _____ ¢ = _____ ¢

⑯   _____ ¢ – _____ ¢ = _____ ¢

⑰  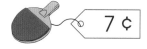 _____ ¢ – _____ ¢ = _____ ¢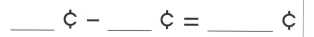

⑱  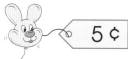 _____ ¢ – _____ ¢ = _____ ¢

The children spent the exact amounts to buy the garage sale items. Write the letters in the boxes to tell what they bought.

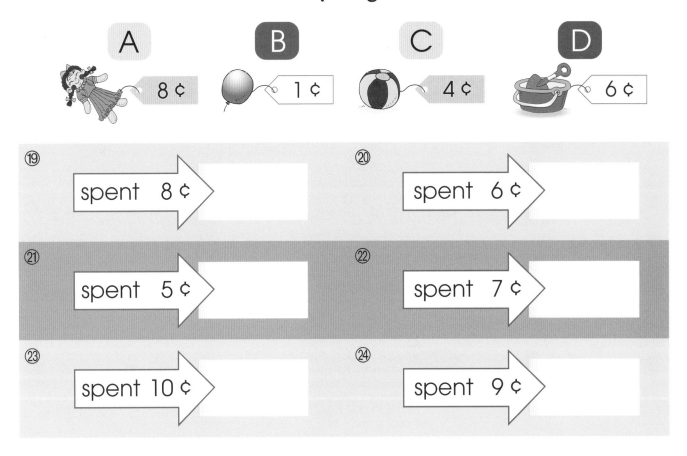

A   8 ¢   B   1 ¢   C   4 ¢   D   6 ¢

⑲ spent 8 ¢   ⑳ spent 6 ¢

㉑ spent 5 ¢   ㉒ spent 7 ¢

㉓ spent 10 ¢   ㉔ spent 9 ¢

Show 3 different ways to make 10¢ with nickels and pennies. Circle the correct number of coins.

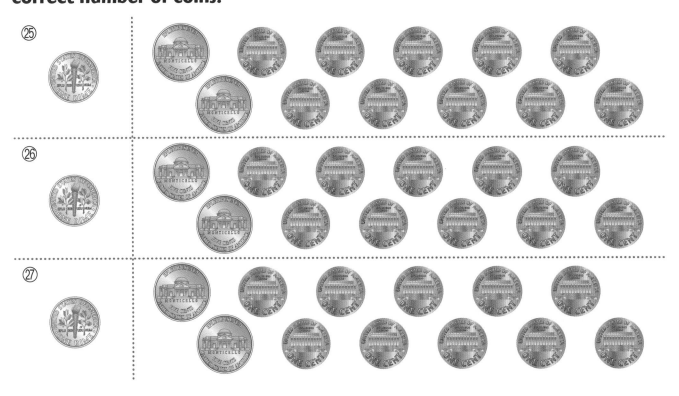

㉕

㉖

㉗

Complete.

3 ¢   1 ¢   4 ¢   5 ¢   6 ¢

㉘ Mom buys 1 and 1 . How much does she pay in all?

_____ = _____   _____ ¢ in all

㉙ Sue buys 1 . Sam buys 1 . How much more does Sue
pay than Sam?

_____ = _____   _____ ¢ more

㉚ Jane buys 1 and 1 . How much does Jane pay in all?

_____ = _____   _____ ¢ in all

㉛ Bob buys 1 . Ben buys 1 . How much more does Bob
pay than Ben?

_____ = _____   _____ ¢ more

㉜ Jack buys 1 , 1 , and 1 . How much does he pay
in all?

_____ = _____   _____ ¢ in all

Just for Fun

Little Frog hops in steps of 2's. Color the path that he follows.

19   20   23   29
18   26
   22
16   21   24   25   28

Add or subtract.

①
$$\begin{array}{r} 12 \\ + 8 \\ \hline \end{array}$$

②
$$\begin{array}{r} 18 \\ - 7 \\ \hline \end{array}$$

③
$$\begin{array}{r} 14 \\ + 4 \\ \hline \end{array}$$

④
$$\begin{array}{r} 19 \\ - 4 \\ \hline \end{array}$$

⑤
$$\begin{array}{r} 17 \\ - 4 \\ \hline \end{array}$$

⑥
$$\begin{array}{r} 11 \\ + 5 \\ \hline \end{array}$$

⑦
$$\begin{array}{r} 13 \\ + 4 \\ \hline \end{array}$$

⑧
$$\begin{array}{r} 18 \\ - 8 \\ \hline \end{array}$$

⑨
$$\begin{array}{r} 14 \\ + 2 \\ \hline \end{array}$$

⑩
$$\begin{array}{r} 16 \\ - 6 \\ \hline \end{array}$$

⑪
$$\begin{array}{r} 20 \\ - 6 \\ \hline \end{array}$$

⑫
$$\begin{array}{r} 17 \\ + 2 \\ \hline \end{array}$$

⑬

-9	
20	
17	
15	
18	

⑭

$+3$	
16	
15	
13	
17	

⑮

-6	
19	
16	
12	
18	

⑯ $8 + 2 + 9 = $ _____

⑰ $3 + 4 + 6 = $ _____

Complete and match. Write the letters in ㉖ to solve the riddle.

⑱ 18 − 2 = _____ N •   • 17 − 2 = _____

⑲ 10 + 4 = _____ A •   • 7 + 4 = _____

⑳ 8 + 7 = _____ D •   • 9 + 7 = _____

㉑ 17 − 6 = _____ O •   • 19 − 5 = _____

㉒ 20 − 7 = _____ U •   • 16 − 4 = _____

㉓ 5 + 12 = _____ I •   • 5 + 8 = _____

㉔ 19 − 7 = _____ S •   • 12 + 6 = _____

㉕ 9 + 9 = _____ R •   • 20 − 3 = _____

Riddle: A large reptile which is extinct.

㉖

15	17	16	11	12	14	13	18

A

Put + or – in the ◯ .

㉗ $12 \bigcirc 7 = 19$

㉘ $16 \bigcirc 4 = 12$

㉙ $11 \bigcirc 6 = 5$

㉚ $8 \bigcirc 3 = 11$

㉛ $13 \bigcirc 5 = 18$

㉜ $15 \bigcirc 2 = 13$

㉝ $6 \bigcirc 8 = 14$

㉞ $10 \bigcirc 6 = 16$

㉟ $14 \bigcirc 5 = 9$

㊱ $7 \bigcirc 6 = 13$

㊲ $18 \bigcirc 6 = 12$

㊳ $13 \bigcirc 9 = 4$

Write the numbers.

㊴ $17 - \boxed{}$

㊵ $2 + \boxed{}$

㊶ $15 - \boxed{}$

㊷ $5 + \boxed{}$

㊸ $12 - \boxed{}$

㊹ $6 + \boxed{}$

㊺ $19 - \boxed{}$

㊻ $4 + \boxed{}$

7

Put the sums of the pairs of cards in order, starting with the smallest number first. Write 1st, 2nd, 3rd, or 4th in the ☐ .

㊼

5 9	6 5	4 8	7 6
A ☐	B ☐	C ☐	D ☐

Complete the number sentences.

⑱
$$6 + 6 = 12$$
a. $6 + 7 = \underline{\hspace{2cm}}$
b. $6 + 8 = \underline{\hspace{2cm}}$
c. $6 + 9 = \underline{\hspace{2cm}}$

⑲
$$14 - 7 = 7$$
a. $15 - 7 = \underline{\hspace{2cm}}$
b. $16 - 7 = \underline{\hspace{2cm}}$
c. $17 - 7 = \underline{\hspace{2cm}}$

Draw and complete.

⑳
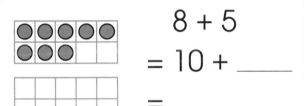
$$8 + 5$$
$$= 10 + \underline{\hspace{1.5cm}}$$
$$= \underline{\hspace{2cm}}$$

㉑
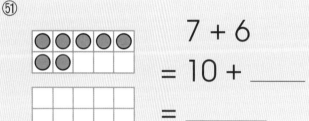
$$7 + 6$$
$$= 10 + \underline{\hspace{1.5cm}}$$
$$= \underline{\hspace{2cm}}$$

Cross out the correct number of items and complete the subtraction sentences.

㉒
$$13 - 6$$
$$= 10 - \underline{\hspace{1.5cm}}$$
$$= \underline{\hspace{2cm}}$$

㉓
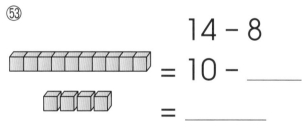
$$14 - 8$$
$$= 10 - \underline{\hspace{1.5cm}}$$
$$= \underline{\hspace{2cm}}$$

Circle the coins needed to buy each item.

㉔
 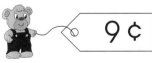 9 ¢

㉕
  7 ¢

Complete.

56 There are 18 🍪 on the table. 6 🍪 roll off.

How many 🍪 are left on the table?

_____ 🍪 left

57 There are 6 🥐 in the box. Mom makes 12 more 🥐 .

How many 🥐 are there in all?

_____ 🥐 in all

58 Sue has 10¢ in all. She buys 1 🏖 ⟨ 5¢ ⟩ .

How much does Sue have left?

_____ ¢ left

59 Sam has 6 🎈 and 5 🎈 .

How many 🎈 🎈 does Sam have altogether?

_____ 🎈 🎈 altogether

60 Bob has 15 🍭 . Ben has 9 🍭 .

How many more 🍭 does Bob have than Ben?

_____ more 🍭

61 Jack buys 1 🚗 7¢ . Jane buys 1 ✈ 9¢ .

How much more does Jane spend than Jack?

_____ ¢ more

Section III

Overview

In Section II, addition and subtraction skills were developed.

In this section, additional opportunities are provided for children to practice these skills in meaningful contexts.

The concepts of shape and symmetry are also developed. Children learn to recognize 2-dimensional shapes such as rectangle, square, triangle, hexagon, and circle, and 3-dimensional shapes such as sphere, prism, cone, cylinder, and pyramid.

In addition, topics such as measurement, money, and graphs are introduced. At this stage, children should be able to use "mathematical language" to express their thinking.

Write the letters in the ☐ **.**

Hello. My name is Jill. I can see many things in the supermarket.

① A.

B.

Light ☐

Heavy ☐

② A.

B.

Big ☐

Small ☐

③ A.

B.

Thick ☐

Thin ☐

④ A.

B.

Straight ☐

Bent ☐

⑤ A.

B.

Short ☐

Long ☐

⑥ A.

B.

More ☐

Fewer ☐

Circle the right answers.

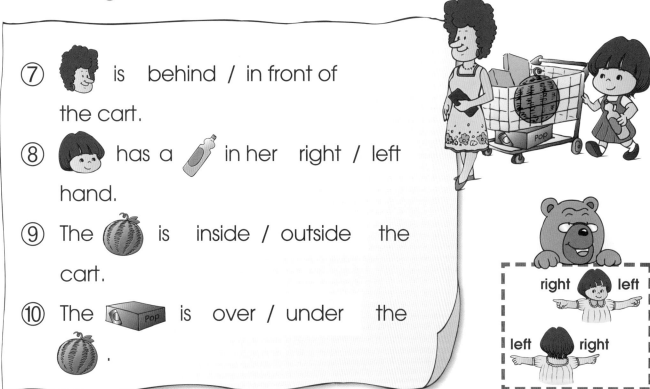

⑦ 🧑 is   behind / in front of

the cart.

⑧ 👧 has a 🍼 in her   right / left

hand.

⑨ The 🍉 is   inside / outside   the

cart.

⑩ The 📦 POP is   over / under   the

🍉 .

Check ✔ the right ☐ .

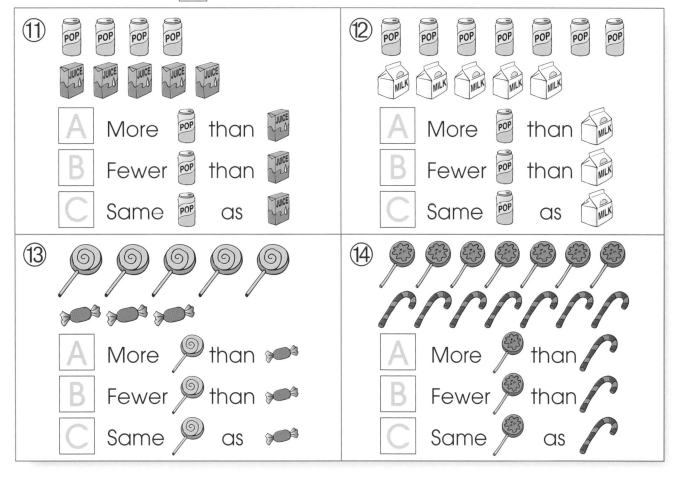

⑪
A   More POP than JUICE

B   Fewer POP than JUICE

C   Same POP as JUICE

⑫
A   More POP than MILK

B   Fewer POP than MILK

C   Same POP as MILK

⑬
A   More 🍭 than 🍬

B   Fewer 🍭 than 🍬

C   Same 🍭 as 🍬

⑭
A   More 🍭 than 🍬

B   Fewer 🍭 than 🍬

C   Same 🍭 as 🍬

Sort the things for Jill. Cross out ✗ the one that does not belong.

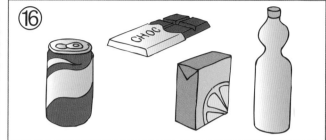

Which comes next? Check ✔ the right ☐ .

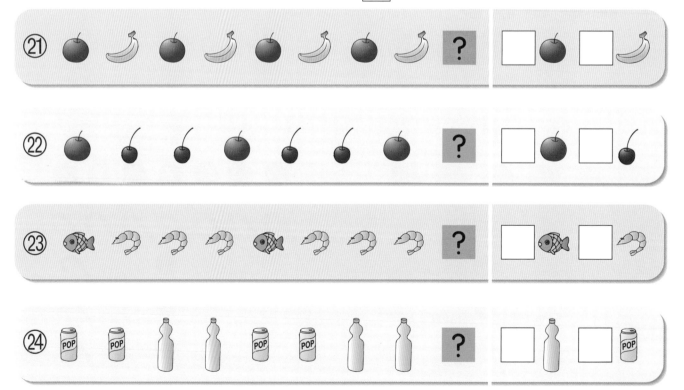

Put the things in order.

㉕ From short to long

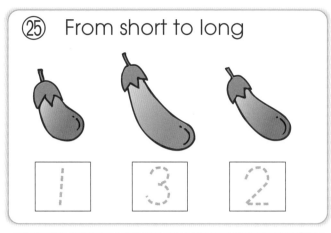

| 1 | 3 | 2 |

㉖ From big to small

㉗ From thin to thick

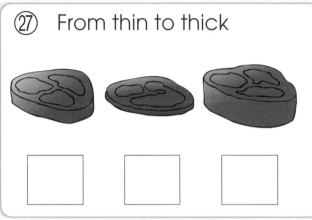

㉘ From narrow to wide

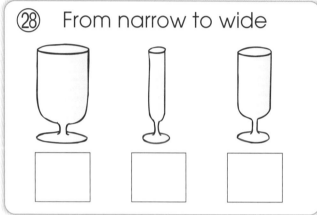

ACTIVITY

Color the things.

1. Color the **taller** light **blue**.
2. Color the **bigger** picture **green**.
3. Color the puppy **behind** the couch **brown**.
4. Color the puppy **under** the couch **yellow**.

2 Numbers 1 - 10

Count and write the numbers.

①  ☐

Numbers 1 to 10

•1	⁝2	⸪3	∷4
⸫⸬5	⸬⸬6	⸬•7	
⸬⸬8	⸬⸬9	⸬10	

②  ☐

③  ☐

④  ☐

Count and color the bones.

⑤ Color the even numbers red.

⑥ Color the odd numbers yellow.

Odd numbers

1	3	5	7	9

Even numbers

2	4	6	8	10

Write the numbers they will walk past.

Count On
Small → Large
e.g. 1, 2, 3, 4, 5 ...
Count Back
Large → Small
e.g. 10, 9, 8, 7, 6 ...

⑦  to 🐕 : 6, ☐ , ☐ , ☐ , 2

⑧ 👦 to 🐭 : 6, ☐ , ☐ , ☐ , 10

⑨ 👧 to 🐕 : 10, ☐ , ☐ , ☐ , ☐ , ☐ ,

☐ , ☐ , ☐ , 1

Circle the right answers.

⑩   is in the 2nd .

→ 🍎 🍐 🍐 🍇 🍌 🍒

The **2nd** and the **3rd** are pears. There are 2 pears.

⑪   is in the 5th .

⑫   is in the 8th .

⑬ How many are there?   7   8   9

Count and write the numbers.

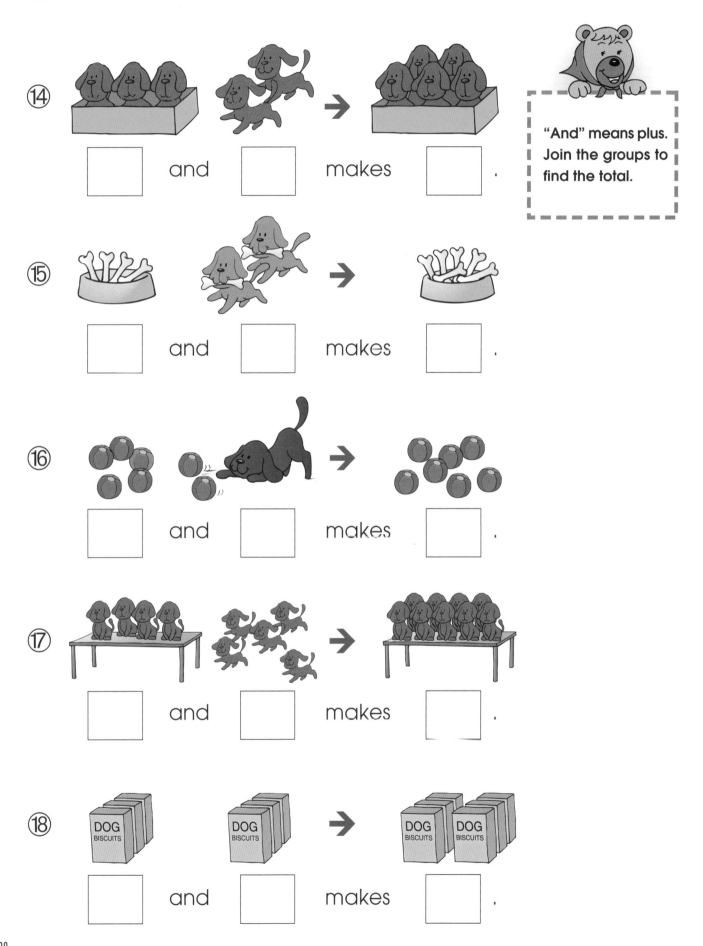

⑭ ☐ and ☐ makes ☐ .

"And" means plus. Join the groups to find the total.

⑮ ☐ and ☐ makes ☐ .

⑯ ☐ and ☐ makes ☐ .

⑰ ☐ and ☐ makes ☐ .

⑱ ☐ and ☐ makes ☐ .

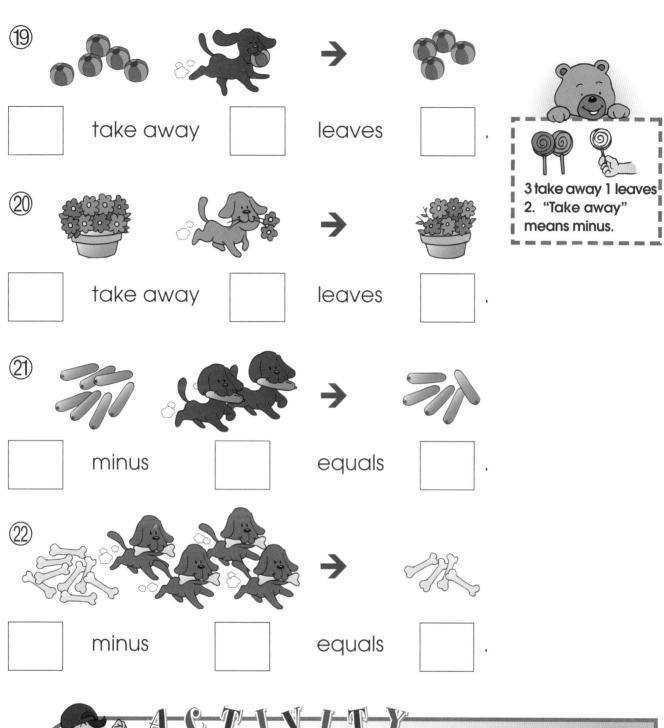

⑲ ☐ take away ☐ leaves ☐ .

3 take away 1 leaves 2. "Take away" means minus.

⑳ ☐ take away ☐ leaves ☐ .

㉑ ☐ minus ☐ equals ☐ .

㉒ ☐ minus ☐ equals ☐ .

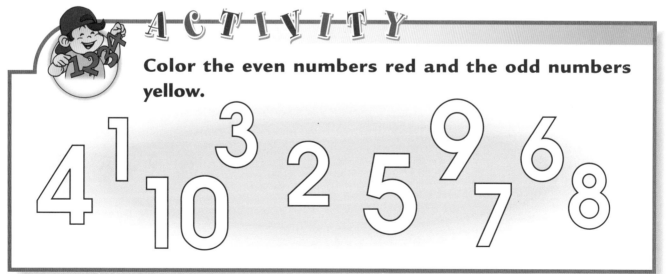

ACTIVITY

Color the even numbers red and the odd numbers yellow.

4 1 3 10 2 5 9 7 6 8

3 Addition and Subtraction

How many stars are there?

① 2 + 3 = ☐

② ☐ + ☐ = ☐

③ ☐ + ☐ = ☐

Numbers must align on the right-hand side, e.g.

$$\begin{array}{r} 2 \\ +3 \\ \hline 5 \end{array}\ \textbf{X} \qquad \begin{array}{r} 2 \\ +3 \\ \hline 5 \end{array}\ \checkmark$$

④ 5
+ 1
☐

⑤ 2
+ 6
☐

⑥ 4
+ 5

⑦ 1
+ 6

⑧ 2
+ 5

⑨ 6
+ 3

⑩ 1 + 9 =

⑪ 5 + 5 =

⑫ 2 + 8 =

⑬ 6 + 4 =

⑭ 9 + 1 =

⑮ 7 + 3 =

Jill and Mark are counting the stars. Write the numbers.

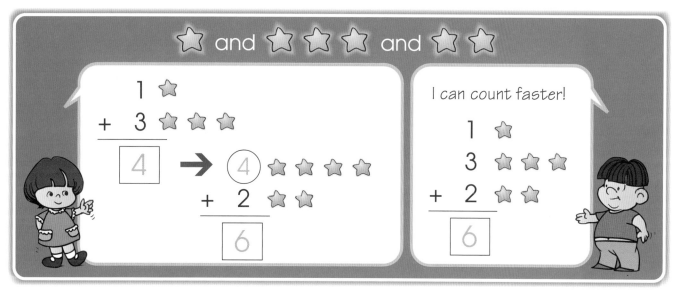

⑯
```
  1  ☆
  2  ☆☆
+ 4  ☆☆☆☆
┌──┐
│  │
└──┘
```

⑰
```
  2  ☆☆
  3  ☆☆☆
+ 3  ☆☆☆
┌──┐
│  │
└──┘
```

⑱
```
  4  ☆☆☆☆
  1  ☆
+ 1  ☆
┌──┐
│  │
└──┘
```

⑲
```
  3
  3
+ 1
```

⑳
```
  2
  3
+ 4
```

㉑
```
  3
  1
+ 4
```

㉒
```
  5
  3
+ 2
```

㉓ **The ☆ with 6 as the answer are Jill's. Color them red.**

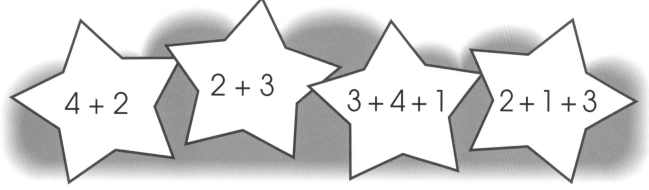

4 + 2   2 + 3   3 + 4 + 1   2 + 1 + 3

131

How many Christmas crackers are left?

㉔　7　－　4　＝ ☐

㉕　5　－ ☐ ＝ ☐

㉖　8
　　－　6
　　☐

㉗　10
　　－ ☐
　　☐

㉘　6
　　－ ☐
　　☐

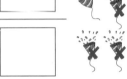

Try these.

㉙　7
　－　6
　☐

㉚　10
　－　7
　☐

㉛　9
　－　5
　☐

Numbers must align on the right-hand side, e.g.

$$\begin{array}{r} 5 \\ -3 \\ \hline 2 \end{array}$$ ✗ $$\begin{array}{r} 5 \\ -3 \\ \hline 2 \end{array}$$ ✔

㉜　8
　－　4
　☐

㉝　6
　－　5
　☐

㉞　10
　－　2
　☐

㉟　7
　－　3
　☐

㊱　7 – 2 = ☐

㊲　8 – 2 = ☐

㊳　9 – 4 = ☐

㊴　8 – 1 = ☐

㊵　5 – 1 = ☐

㊶　6 – 4 = ☐

Read what they say. Write the numbers.

(42) I have 5  . Mom gave me 2 more  .

Now I have ☐ .

(43) I have 2 ⚫ and 2 ⚫ .

I have ☐ ⚫⚫ in all.

(44) I have 8 🧱 . I gave 2 to 👧 . Now I

have ☐ 🧱 .

(45) 👧 has 9 📘 . I have 5 📘 .

👧 has ☐ 📘 more than me.

(46) We had 7 🎈 but 3 💥 burst.

Now we have ☐ 🎈 left.

ACTIVITY

Which pairs of numbers make 10? Color them with the same color.

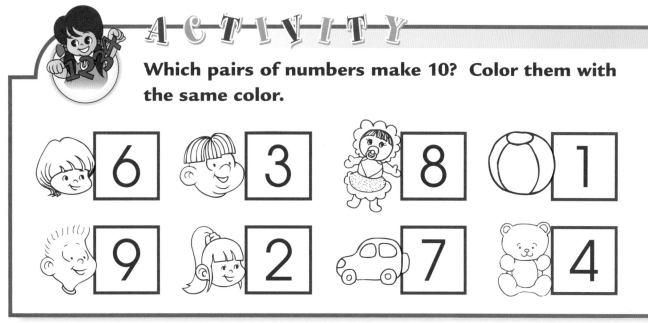

| 6 | 3 | 8 | 1 |
| 9 | 2 | 7 | 4 |

Count and write the number of toys. Circle the right words.

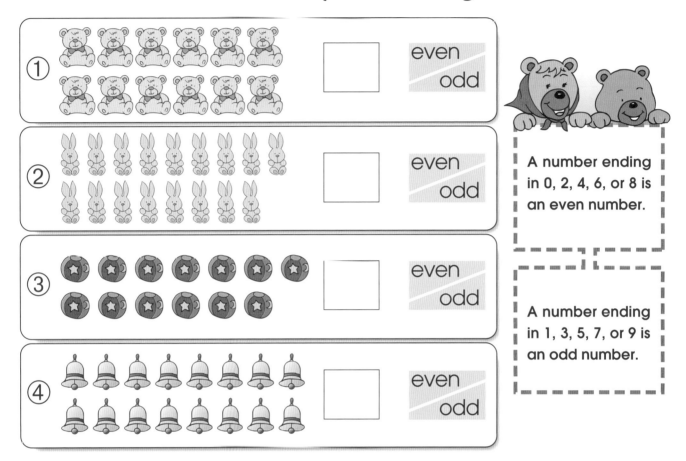

① even / odd

② even / odd

③ even / odd

④ even / odd

A number ending in 0, 2, 4, 6, or 8 is an even number.

A number ending in 1, 3, 5, 7, or 9 is an odd number.

Help Jill throw the balls. Write the numbers.

⑤ Odd Numbers

⑥ Even Numbers

12

Fill in the numbers.

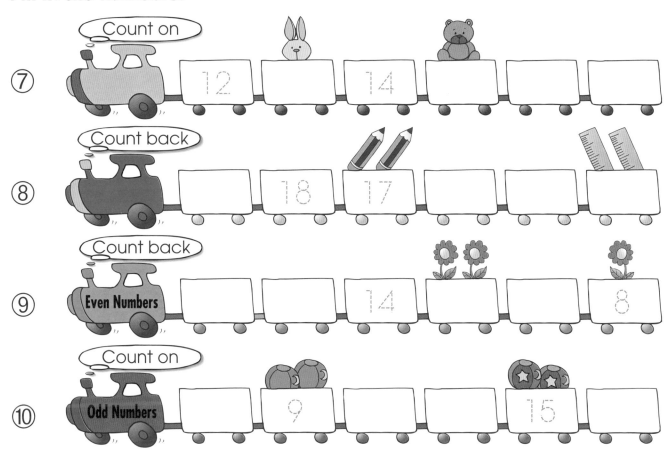

Check ✔ the gifts.

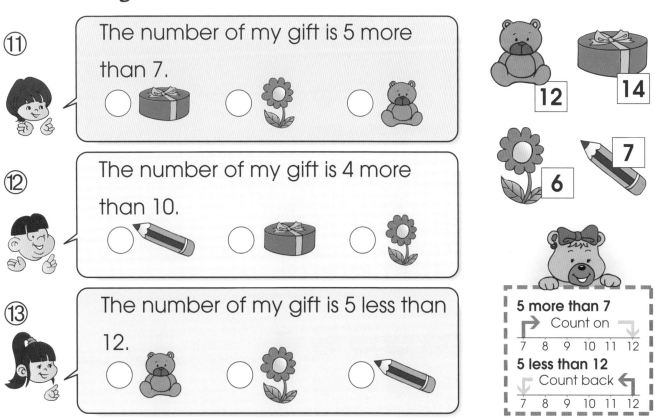

⑪ The number of my gift is 5 more than 7.
○ 🎁 ○ 🌸 ○ 🧸

⑫ The number of my gift is 4 more than 10.
○ ✏️ ○ 🎁 ○ 🌸

⑬ The number of my gift is 5 less than 12.
○ 🧸 ○ 🌸 ○ ✏️

12 14
6 7

5 more than 7
➡ Count on ⬇
7 8 9 10 11 12
5 less than 12
⬇ Count back ⬅
7 8 9 10 11 12

Help Jill draw the lines. Write the numbers.

There is 1 group of 10 and 1 group of 5.

⑭

$$15 = 10 + 5$$

⑮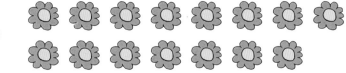

$$15 = \boxed{} + 3$$

⑯

$$\boxed{} = 8 + \boxed{}$$

⑰

$$17 = 6 + \boxed{}$$

⑱

$$\boxed{} = \boxed{} + 9$$

⑲

$$\boxed{} = 10 + \boxed{}$$

⑳

$$\boxed{} = 4 + \boxed{}$$

Write the numbers.

Find how much food we had.

Any number plus 0 equals itself, e.g.

$$5 + 0 = \underline{5}$$

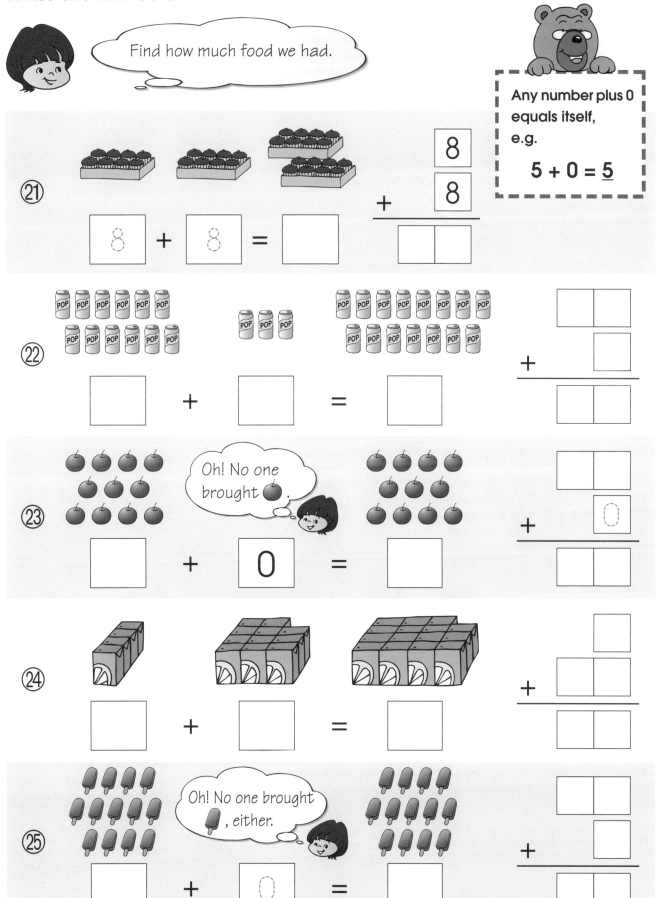

㉑ 8 + 8 = ☐

㉒ ☐ + ☐ = ☐

㉓ ☐ + 0 = ☐

Oh! No one brought 🍎.

㉔ ☐ + ☐ = ☐

㉕ ☐ + 0 = ☐

Oh! No one brought 🍦, either.

Write the numbers.

Find how much food is left.

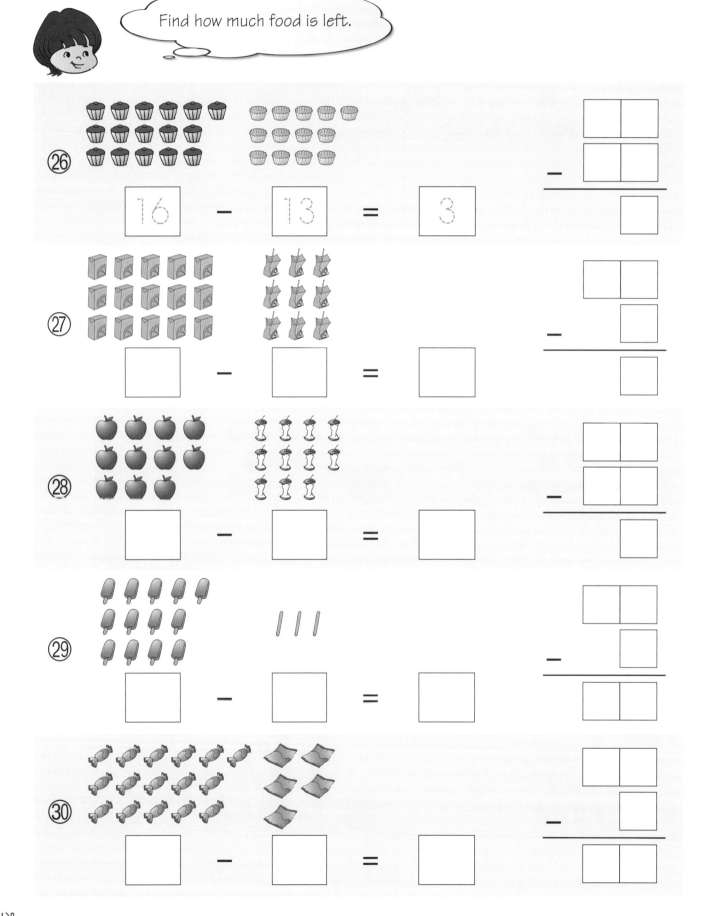

26) 16 – 13 = 3

27) [ ] – [ ] = [ ]

28) [ ] – [ ] = [ ]

29) [ ] – [ ] = [ ]

30) [ ] – [ ] = [ ]

Read what Jill and Mark say. Write the numbers.

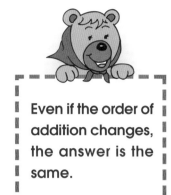

Even if the order of addition changes, the answer is the same.

2 + 3 = 3 + 2

㉛ $3 + 4 = \boxed{} + 3$

㉜ $5 + \boxed{} = 2 + 5$

㉝ $\boxed{} + 1 = 1 + 8$

㉞ $1 + 4 = \boxed{} + 1$

㉟ $3 + \boxed{} = 1 + 3$

㊱ $2 + 6 = 6 + \boxed{}$

ACTIVITY

Write the missing numbers.

1. $9 - \boxed{} = 7$

2. $6 + \boxed{} = 13$

3. $5 - \boxed{} = 4$

4. $2 + \boxed{} = 16$

5. $\boxed{} - 4 = 7$

6. $\boxed{} - 2 = 4$

1   14   7   6   11

Solids

Put Jill's things in the right boxes. Write the letters only.

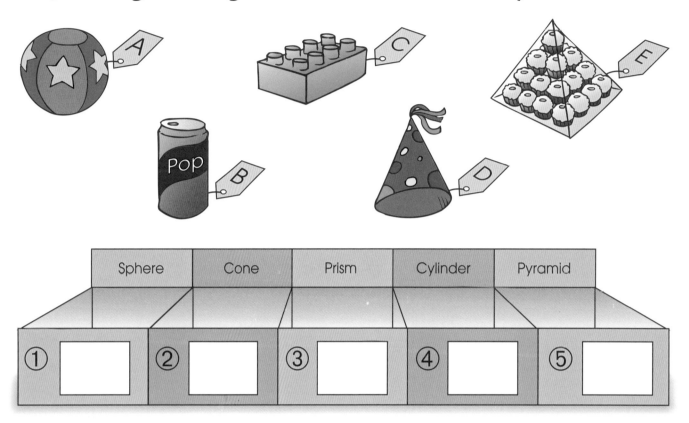

Sphere	Cone	Prism	Cylinder	Pyramid
①	②	③	④	⑤

In each group, circle the shape that is not the same. Check ✔ the name of the other shapes.

⑥ □ Pyramid □ Sphere □ Prism

⑦ □ Cylinder □ Prism □ Cone

⑧ □ Cone □ Sphere □ Cylinder

⑨
- ☐ Cylinder
- ☐ Cone
- ☐ Pyramid

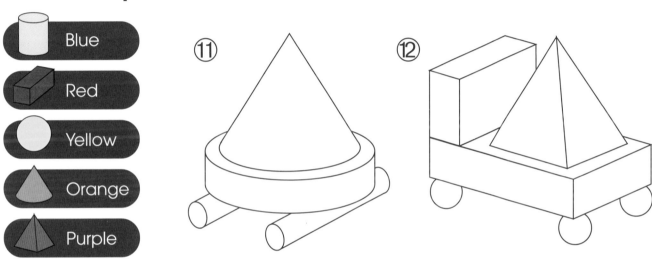

⑩
- ☐ Sphere
- ☐ Cone
- ☐ Cylinder

Color the shapes.

- Blue
- Red
- Yellow
- Orange
- Purple

⑪

⑫

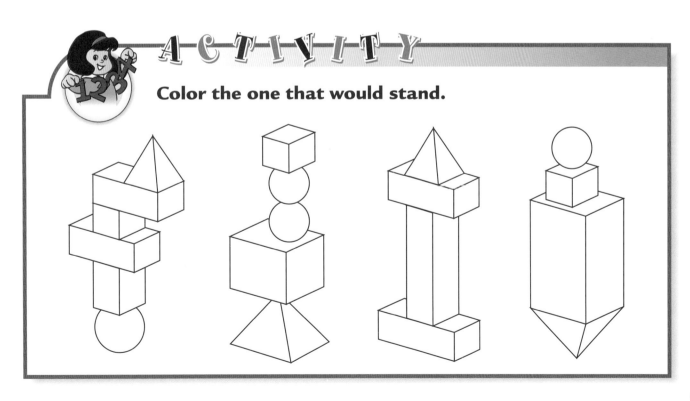

ACTIVITY

Color the one that would stand.

Solid Column Graphs

Jill and Mark are building towers. Circle the right answers.

① How many blocks does have? | 6 | 7 | 9

② How many blocks does have? | 7 | 8 | 9

③ Whose tower has more blocks?

④ How many more blocks? | 1 | 2 | 3

Sort Jill's beads by color. Draw them on the posts.

Cross out ✗ each bead as you draw it.

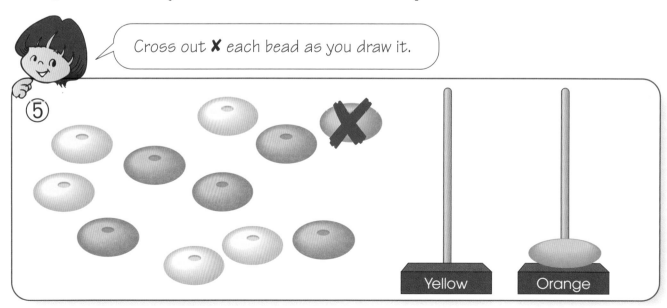

⑤

Yellow   Orange

Write the answers.

⑥ How many ![bead] ? ▢

⑦ How many ![bead] ? ▢

⑧ Which post has more beads? ▭

⑨ How many more? ▢

Check ✔ the right answers.

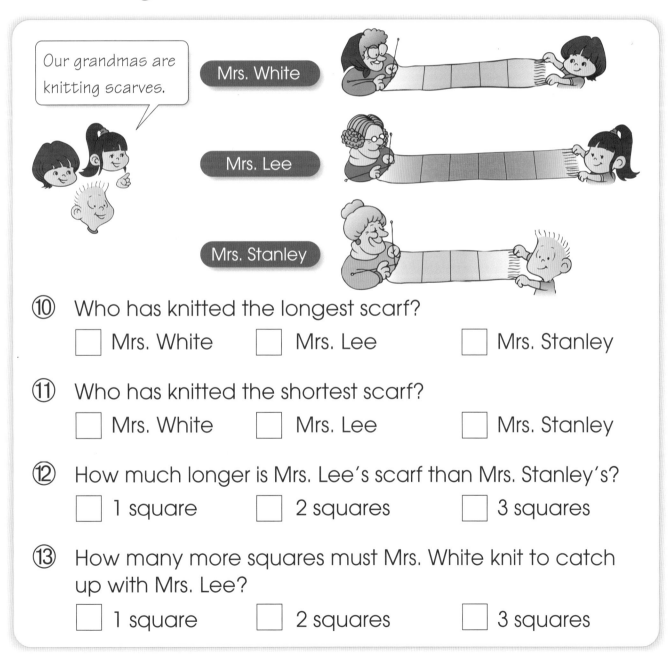

Our grandmas are knitting scarves.

Mrs. White

Mrs. Lee

Mrs. Stanley

⑩ Who has knitted the longest scarf?

☐ Mrs. White ☐ Mrs. Lee ☐ Mrs. Stanley

⑪ Who has knitted the shortest scarf?

☐ Mrs. White ☐ Mrs. Lee ☐ Mrs. Stanley

⑫ How much longer is Mrs. Lee's scarf than Mrs. Stanley's?

☐ 1 square ☐ 2 squares ☐ 3 squares

⑬ How many more squares must Mrs. White knit to catch up with Mrs. Lee?

☐ 1 square ☐ 2 squares ☐ 3 squares

Jill, Mark, and David go fishing. Fill in the ☐ .

⑭ has ☐ 🐟 .

⑮ has ☐ 🐟 .

⑯ has ☐ 🐟 .

Jill   David   Mark

⑰ They have ☐ 🐟 in all.

⑱ Jill has as many 🐟 as ☐ .

⑲ Mark has more 🐟 than ☐ . He has ☐ more.

⑳ Who has the fewest 🐟 ? ☐

The graph shows the number of balls the children have. Fill in the ☐ .

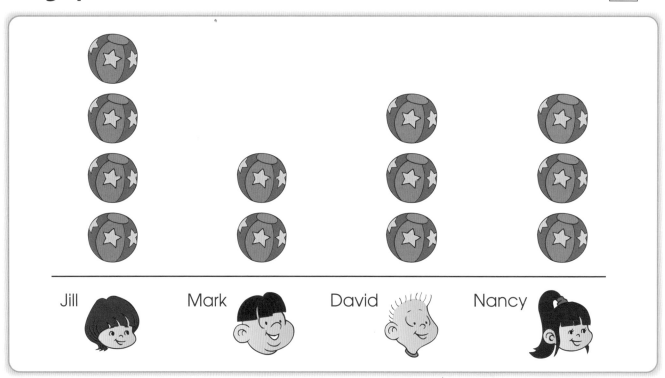

Jill   Mark   David   Nancy

㉑ has [ ] balls.

㉒ has [ ] balls.

㉓ [   ] has the most balls.

㉔ [   ] has the fewest balls.

㉕ [   ] and [   ] have the same number

of balls.

㉖ The children have [ ] balls in all.

ACTIVITY

Complete the graph and answer the questions.

1. Color 1 box for one child.

2. How many girls? [ ]   3. How many boys? [ ]

4. How many children? [ ]   5. How many more boys than girls? [ ]

Look at the lockers. Do questions 1 to 4.

① Write the missing numbers.

②  has a 🧒 on her locker door. Her locker number is ☐ .

③  has a 🐱 on his locker door. His locker number is ☐ .

④ Write from large to small the numbers of the opened lockers.

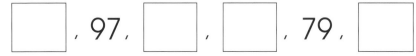

☐ , 97 , ☐ , ☐ , 79 , ☐

Fill in the missing numbers.

⑤  | | 38 | | | 41 | | |

⑥ | | 25 | | | 22 | | |

⑦  | | | 48 | 49 | | | |

⑧ | 92 | | | | | 87 | |

Count and write the numbers.

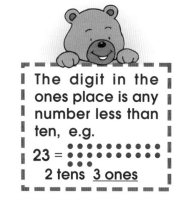

The digit in the ones place is any number less than ten, e.g.

$23 = $
2 tens 3 ones

⑨ 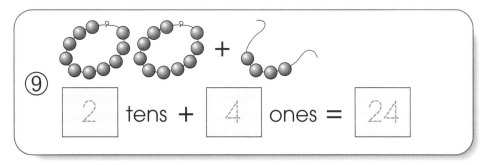 ⎡2⎤ tens + ⎡4⎤ ones = ⎡24⎤

⑩ + [ ] tens + [ ] ones = [ ]

⑪ + [ ] tens + [ ] ones = [ ]

⑫ + [ ] tens + [ ] ones = [ ]

147

Circle the better estimates. Count and write how many in the ☐ .

⑬

more than 30	
fewer than 30	

⑭

more than 40	
fewer than 40	

⑮

more than 50	
fewer than 50	

⑯

more than 60	
fewer than 60	

Circle the marbles in groups of ten. Write the numbers.

⑰

23   twenty-three

⑱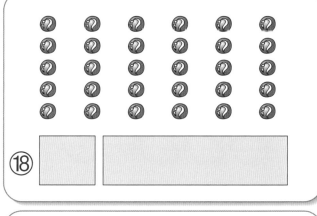

⑲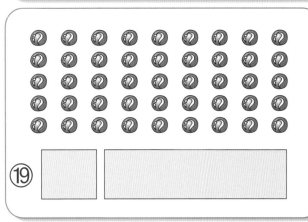

⑳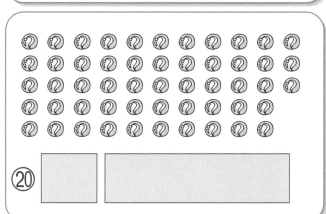

Count the blocks. Draw the beads and write the numbers.

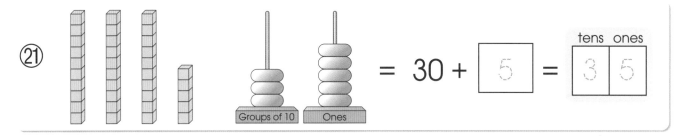

㉑ = 30 + [5] = | tens: 3 | ones: 5 |

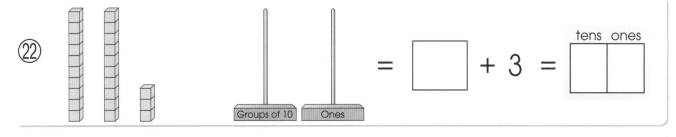

㉒ = [ ] + 3 = | tens | ones |

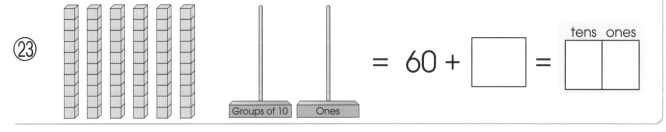

㉓ = 60 + [ ] = | tens | ones |

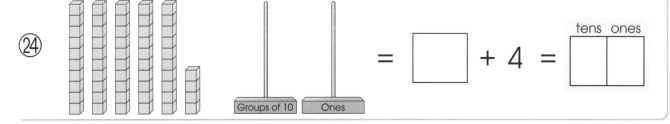

㉔ = [ ] + 4 = | tens | ones |

Color the even numbers yellow and the odd numbers green.

㉕

If the last digit of a number is 1,3,5,7, or 9, it is an odd number. If it is 2,4, 6, 8, or 0, it is an even number.

62 30 66
21 55 95
44 49 53
37 86

Fill in the ☐ **.**

㉖ 36 = ☐ tens and ☐ ones = ☐ + 6

㉗ 49 = ☐ tens and ☐ ones = ☐ + 9

㉘ 61 = ☐ tens and ☐ ones = 60 + ☐

㉙ 75 = ☐ tens and ☐ ones = 70 + ☐

㉚ 90 = ☐ tens and ☐ ones = 90 + ☐

㉛ 9 = ☐ tens and ☐ ones = ☐ + 9

Count the 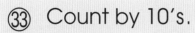 **by 5's and 10's. Write the numbers.**

㉜ Count by 5's.

5, 10, ☐ , ☐ , ☐ , ☐ ,

☐ , 40, ☐ , ☐ , ☐ , ☐

㉝ Count by 10's.

10, 20, ☐ , ☐ , ☐ , ☐

㉞ Circle the faster way to count.

by 5's   by 10's

Count the flowers by 2's, 5's, and 10's. Write the numbers.

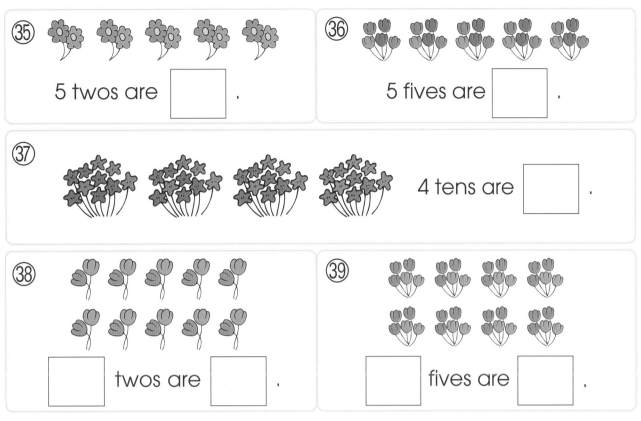

㉟ 5 twos are ☐ .

㊱ 5 fives are ☐ .

㊲ 4 tens are ☐ .

㊳ ☐ twos are ☐ .

㊴ ☐ fives are ☐ .

ACTIVITY

Count by 10's. Color the stones that Jill can step on to cross the river.

25   70   95
85   100
5   75
10   80
20
50   70   90
30   50
40   25   100
40   60
45   35   50   80

10
+10 ↓
20
+10 ↓
30
+10 ↓

Write the letters. (2 marks)

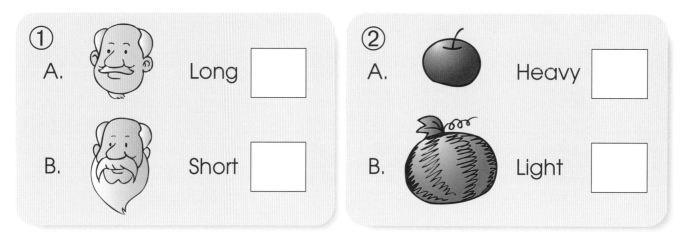

1.
A. Long ☐
B. Short ☐

2.
A. Heavy ☐
B. Light ☐

Cross out X the thing that is different. (4 marks)

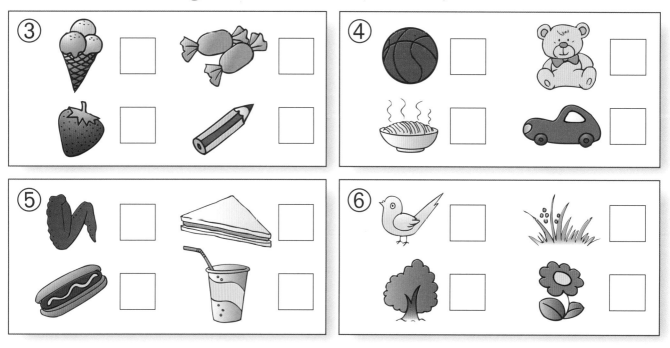

Which comes next? Circle the right pictures. (2 marks)

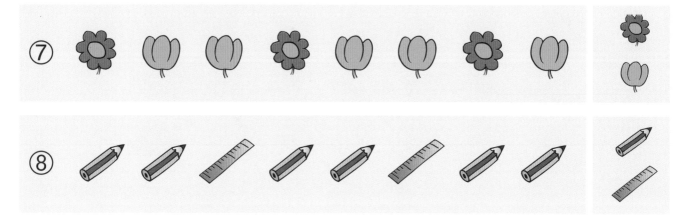

7.

8.

Circle the right children. (6 marks)

⑨ Who is the 1st?

⑩ Who is the 3rd?

⑪ Who is the 5th?

Write the numbers. (38 marks)

⑫ ☐ + ☐ = ☐

⑬ ☐ − ☐ = ☐

⑭ ☐ + ☐ + ☐ = ☐

⑮
$$17 - 4 = \boxed{}$$

⑯
$$8 - 8 = \boxed{}$$

⑰
$$15 + 0 = \boxed{}$$

⑱
$$\begin{array}{r} 2 \\ 2 \\ + 5 \\ \hline \boxed{} \end{array}$$

⑲
$$\begin{array}{r} 1 \\ 4 \\ + 2 \\ \hline \boxed{} \end{array}$$

⑳
$$\begin{array}{r} 3 \\ 1 \\ + 4 \\ \hline \boxed{} \end{array}$$

㉑ $9 + 2 = \boxed{}$

㉒ $16 - 2 = \boxed{}$

㉓ $13 + 6 = \boxed{}$

㉔ $2 + 12 = \boxed{}$

㉕ $15 - 4 = \boxed{}$

㉖ $17 - 17 = \boxed{}$

㉗ 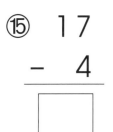 has 5 🏀 . 🙂 has 13 🏀 .
They have $\boxed{}$ 🏀 in all.

㉘ 15 boys and 9 girls are in the playground.
There are $\boxed{}$ more boys.

㉙ There were 14 🌼 in the vase. 🙂 put in 2 more 🌼 .
There are $\boxed{}$ 🌼 in the vase now.

㉚ 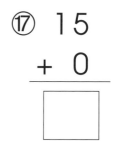 has 5 🍦 . 🙂 has 5 🍦 and 🙂 has 5 🍦 .
They have $\boxed{}$ 🍦 in all.

Write the letters. (8 marks)

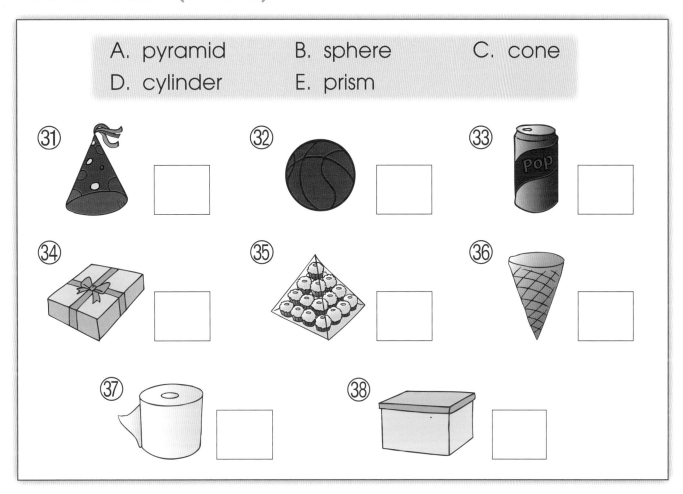

A. pyramid   B. sphere   C. cone
D. cylinder   E. prism

㉛ ☐

㉜ ☐

㉝ ☐

㉞ ☐

㉟ ☐

㊱ ☐

㊲ ☐

㊳ ☐

Color the correct number of  **and fill in the** ☐ . (4 marks)

㊴ has 5 . has 8 and has 6 .

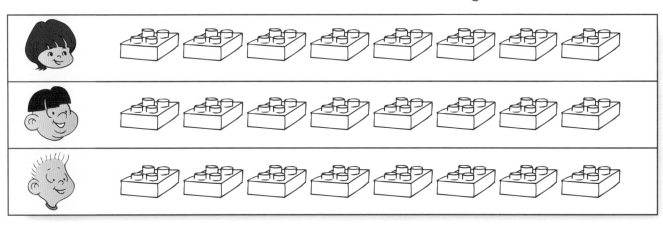

㊵ has ☐ more than .

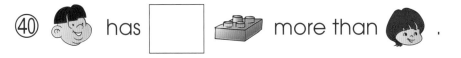

How many beads? Count and write. (4 marks)

㊶ There are ___ blue beads.

㊷ There are ___ red beads.

㊸ There are ___ more blue beads.

㊹ There are ___ beads in all.

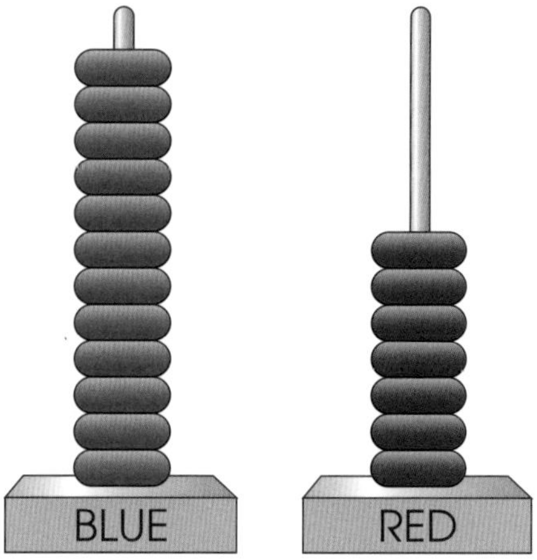

Write A for even numbers and B for odd numbers. (10 marks)

㊺ 75 ___

㊻ 92 ___

㊼ 39 ___

㊽ 67 ___

㊾ twenty-eight ___

㊿ thirteen ___

(51) seventy-one ___

(52) forty-four ___

(53) sixty ___

(54) ninety-six ___

Write the numbers in order from the largest to the smallest. (4 marks)

(55) 52 26 17 43 40 50

___ , ___ , ___ , ___ , ___ , ___

(56) 36 29 15 41 30 20

___ , ___ , ___ , ___ , ___ , ___

Write the missing numbers. (12 marks)

㊗ 39 = ☐ + 9   ㊘ 62 = ☐ + 2

㊙ 99 = 90 + ☐   ⑥⓪ 30 = 30 + ☐

⑥① 86 = ☐ + 6   ⑥② 14 = ☐ + 4

⑥③ 5 = ☐ + 5   ⑥④ 80 = ☐ + 0

⑥⑤ 4 + 5 = ☐ + 4   ⑥⑥ 8 + 9 = ☐ + 8

⑥⑦ 9 + 4 = 4 + ☐   ⑥⑧ ☐ + 6 = 6 + 5

Continue the patterns. (6 marks)

⑥⑨ 40, 50, 60, ☐ , ☐ , ☐

⑦⓪ 65, 70, 75, ☐ , ☐ , ☐

⑦① 13, 15, 17, ☐ , ☐ , ☐

⑦② 35, 40, 45, ☐ , ☐ , ☐

⑦③ 68, 70, 72, ☐ , ☐ , ☐

⑦④ 54, 56, 58, ☐ , ☐ , ☐

SCORE

100

157

8 More about Addition and Subtraction

Help Jill count her toys. Write the numbers in the ☐ .

Adding 2-digit numbers:

1st Add the ones column.

2nd Add the tens column.

```
  2 5        2 5        2 5
+ 1 3      + 1 3      + 1 3
─────      ─────      ─────
 ☐ ☐   1st   ☐ 8  2nd   3 8
```

①

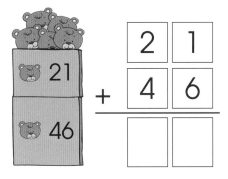

```
  3 2
+ 1 1
─────
 ☐ ☐
```

Numbers must align on the right-hand side, e.g.

```
 3 2        3 2
+1 1        + 1 1
─────  ✗    ─────  ✔
 4 3         4 3
```

②

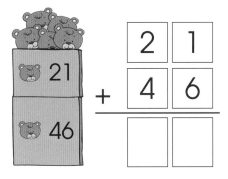

```
  2 1
+ 4 6
─────
 ☐ ☐
```

③

```
 ▨ 8
+ 7 0
─────
 ☐ ☐
```

Put the numbers in the right columns, tens to tens, and ones to ones, e.g.

```
   8         8
+ 7 0      + 7 0
─────  ✗   ─────  ✔
 7 8         7 8
```

Try these.

④ 32 + 46 = ☐

⑤ 28 + 51 = ☐

⑥ 62 + 5 = ☐

⑦ 35 + 24 = ☐

Help Jill count the fruit she picked. Write the numbers in the ☐ .

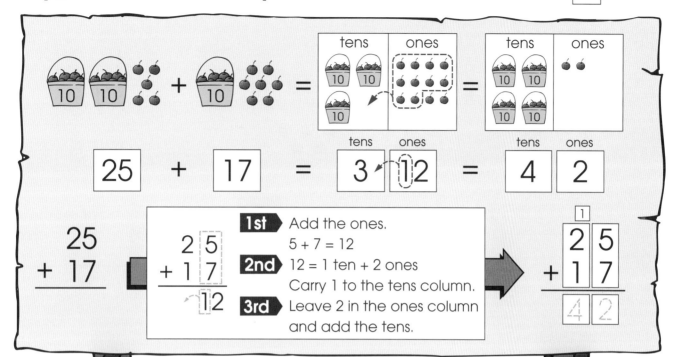

$$25 \quad + \quad 17 \quad = \quad 3 \, 12 \quad = \quad 4 \, 2$$

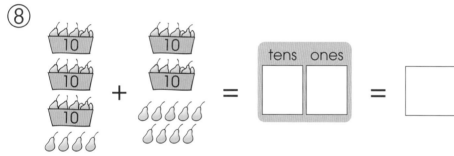

25
+ 17

	2	5
+	1	7
	1	2

1st ▶ Add the ones.
5 + 7 = 12

2nd ▶ 12 = 1 ten + 2 ones
Carry 1 to the tens column.

3rd ▶ Leave 2 in the ones column
and add the tens.

	1	
	2	5
+	1	7
	4	2

⑧

+ =

tens	ones

= ☐

	☐	
	3	4
+	2	9

Try these.

⑨

	☐	
	2	8
+	5	6

⑩

	☐	
	3	7
+	4	9

⑪

	☐	
	1	2
+	7	8

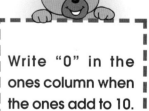

Write "0" in the
ones column when
the ones add to 10.

⑫ 9 + 55 = ☐

⑬ 67 + 8 = ☐

⑭ 18 + 18 = ☐

⑮ 27 + 13 = ☐

159

Count the apples and write the numbers in the ☐ **.**

⑯

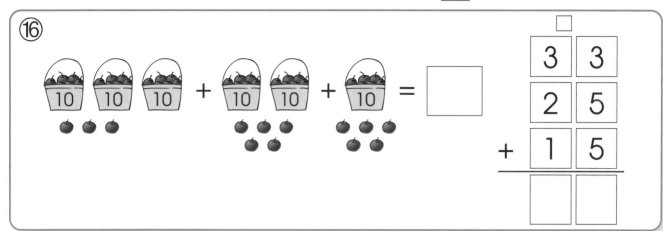

⑰ ⑱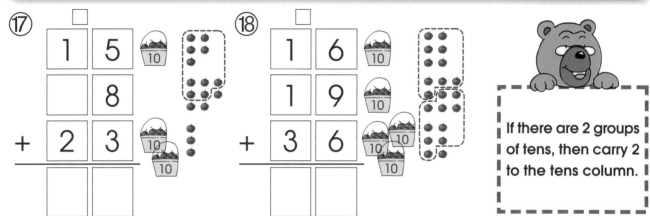

If there are 2 groups of tens, then carry 2 to the tens column.

Try these.

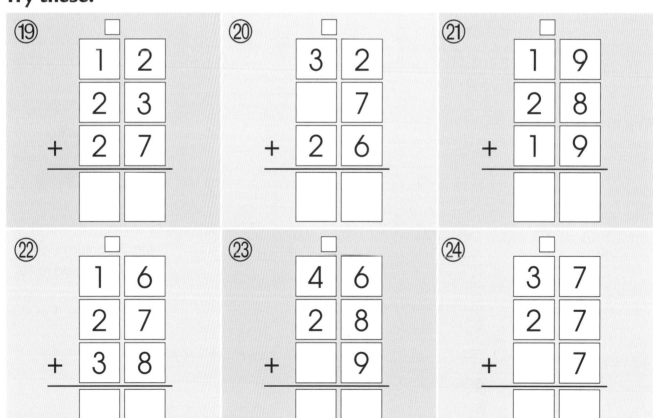

Jill gave Nancy some of her beads. Help her count the beads left. Write the numbers in the **.**

㉕

$$48 - 15 = \boxed{}$$

㉖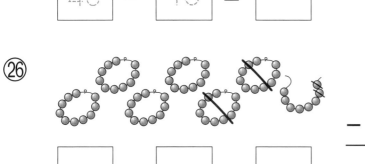

$$\boxed{} - \boxed{} = \boxed{}$$

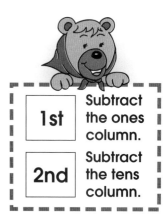

	Subtract the ones column.
1st	Subtract the ones column.
2nd	Subtract the tens column.

Try these.

Don't forget to write "0" under the ones column, e.g.

```
  3 8
-   8
  3 0
```
You have to write "0" here.

If the first number is zero, you can leave it out,
e.g.
```
  3 8
- 3 0
    8
```
Leave "0" out.

㉗
```
  3 6
- 1 4
```

㉘
```
  5 8
- 1 6
```

㉙
```
  7 7
- 5 4
```

㉚
```
  8 6
- 7 1
```

㉛
```
  6 5
- 4 5
```

㉜
```
  4 9
- 3 2
```

㉝
```
  5 2
- 5 0
```

㉞
```
  1 2
- 1 2
```

㉟
```
  3 6
- 3 0
```

㊱
```
  3 8
- 3 8
```

Read what the children say. Write the number sentences.

37 There are 13 and 16 in my class. How many children are there?

☐ + ☐ = ☐

There are ☐ and in all.

38 There are 36 , 21 , and 16 in the playground. How many children are there?

☐ + ☐ + ☐ = ☐

There are ☐ children.

39 Our teacher bought us 39 POP . We drank 29 POP . How many POP were left?

☐ – ☐ = ☐

☐ POP were left.

ACTIVITY

Write the answers in the ☐. Link the children with the same number.

1.
```
  58
-　14
```
A

2.
```
  39
-　 5
```
B

3.
```
  23
+ 33
```
C

4.
```
  15
+ 10
```
D

5.
```
  22
+ 25
```
E

6.
```
   8
  16
+ 32
```
F

7.
```
  39
- 14
```
G

8.
```
  16
+ 28
```
H

9.
```
  59
- 25
```
I

10.
```
   9
  15
+ 23
```
J

11.

Measurement

Match the words with the pictures.

①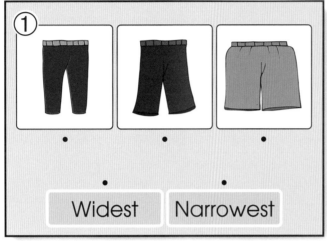

Widest   Narrowest

②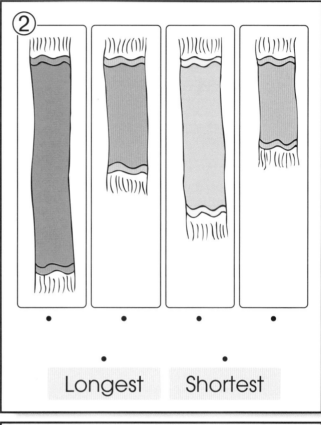

Longest   Shortest

③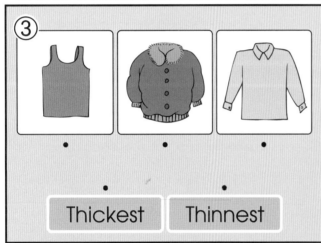

Thickest   Thinnest

⑤

Tallest   Shortest

④

Heaviest   Lightest

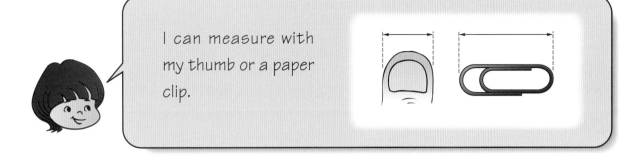

I can measure with my thumb or a paper clip.

How many thumbs and paper clips? Write the numbers.

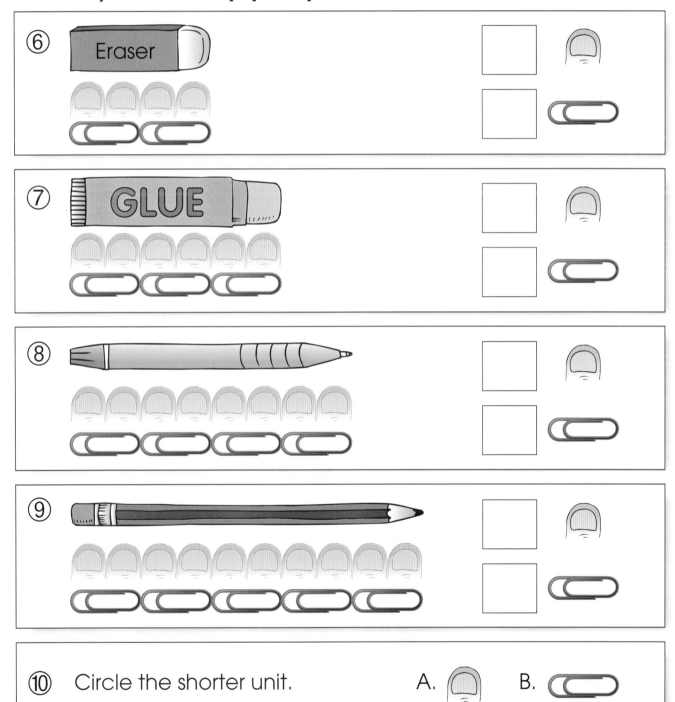

⑥ Eraser

⑦ GLUE

⑧

⑨

⑩ Circle the shorter unit. A.   B.

How long are they? Write the answers in the ☐ .

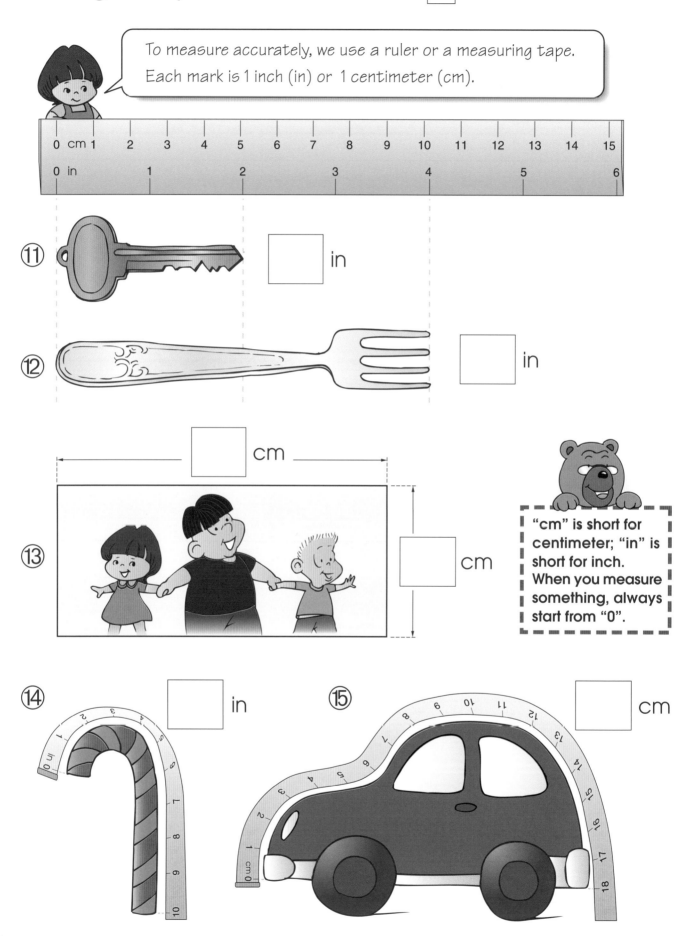

To measure accurately, we use a ruler or a measuring tape.
Each mark is 1 inch (in) or 1 centimeter (cm).

⑪ ☐ in

⑫ ☐ in

⑬ ☐ cm ☐ cm

"cm" is short for centimeter; "in" is short for inch. When you measure something, always start from "0".

⑭ ☐ in ⑮ ☐ cm

Sometimes we can't get exact readings. Measure these worms.

Check ✔ the right answers.

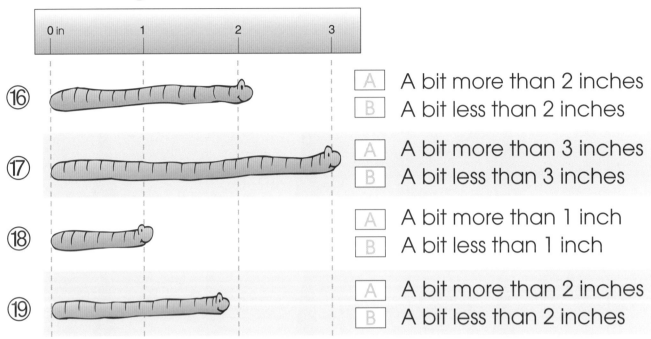

⑯
A □ A bit more than 2 inches
B □ A bit less than 2 inches

⑰
A □ A bit more than 3 inches
B □ A bit less than 3 inches

⑱
A □ A bit more than 1 inch
B □ A bit less than 1 inch

⑲
A □ A bit more than 2 inches
B □ A bit less than 2 inches

Estimate and count. Write the numbers.

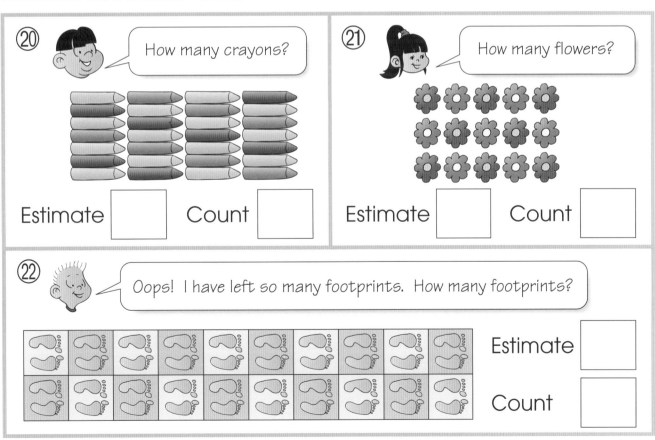

⑳ How many crayons?

Estimate ☐   Count ☐

㉑ How many flowers?

Estimate ☐   Count ☐

㉒ Oops! I have left so many footprints. How many footprints?

Estimate ☐

Count ☐

Color the reasonable pictures.

㉓

㉔

㉕

In each group, color the one that holds the most water.

㉖

㉗

㉘

Write the numbers.

Can you tell me the weight of my things?

29

A 🚗 has the same weight as [ ] 🧱 .

30

A 📦 has the same weight as [ ] 🧱 .

ACTIVITY

Measure and color.

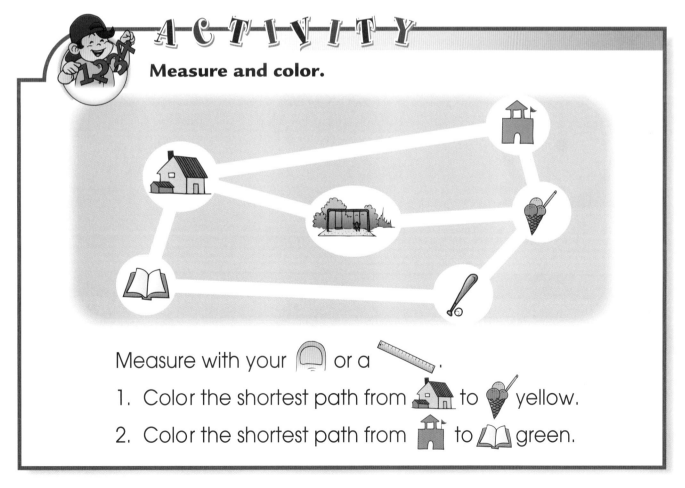

Measure with your 🖐 or a 📏 .

1. Color the shortest path from 🏠 to 🍦 yellow.

2. Color the shortest path from 🏰 to 📖 green.

10 Time

Jill has a new clock. Read what she says.

The long hand is the minute hand.
The short hand is the hour hand.

It is <u>three o'clock</u> when the hour hand points to 3 and the minute hand points to 12.

It is <u>half past two</u> when the hour hand is between 2 and 3 and the minute hand points to 6.

Help Jill write the times.

①

[ ] o'clock

②

[ ] o'clock

③

[ ] o'clock

④

half past [ ]

⑤

half past [ ]

⑥

half past [ ]

Draw the clock hands.

⑦ I wake up at seven o'clock in the morning.

⑧ I have lunch at half past twelve.

⑨ I go home at half past three.

Check ✔ the right answers.

The minute hand is <u>past</u> 12. It is <u>a little after</u> 3 o'clock.

The minute hand <u>has not reached</u> 6. It is <u>nearly</u> half past 9.

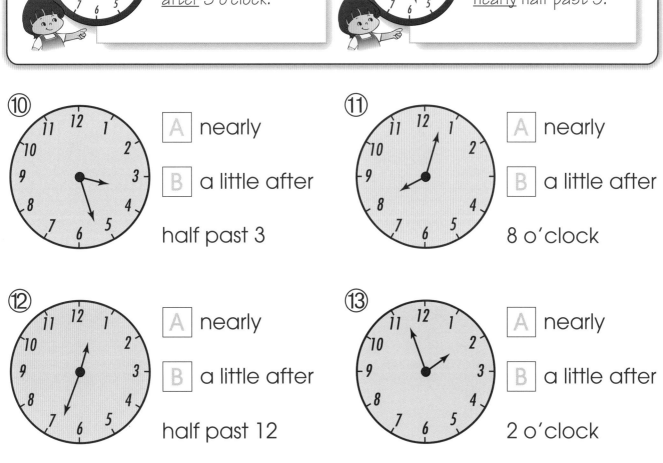

⑩
A nearly
B a little after
half past 3

⑪
A nearly
B a little after
8 o'clock

⑫
A nearly
B a little after
half past 12

⑬
A nearly
B a little after
2 o'clock

See what Jill will do next week. Fill in the blanks.

Sunday	Monday	Tuesday	Wednesday	Thursday	Friday	Saturday

⑭ When will Jill go to ?

⑮ When will Jill play ?

⑯ When will Jill go to ?

⑰ When will Jill go to ?

⑱ There are ☐ days in a week.

Sunday is the first day of a week.

Saturday is the last day of a week.

Look at Jill's calendar. Color the months that match the seasons.

January	February	March	April	May	June

July	August	September	October	November	December

⑲ Color winter blue.

⑳ Color spring green.

㉑ Color summer red.

㉒ Color fall yellow.

172

Check ✔ the temperature that matches the season.

㉓ Winter

    A Coldest   B Warmest   C Getting colder

㉔ Spring

    A Warmest   B Getting warmer   C Getting colder

㉕ Summer

    A Getting warmer   B Warmest   C Coldest

㉖ Fall

    A Getting warmer   B Coldest   C Getting colder

See what Jill did last year.

㉗ Put the seasons in order starting with winter.

ACTIVITY

Write the missing dates and do the coloring.

AUGUST

Sunday	Monday	Tuesday	Wednesday	Thursday	Friday	Saturday
	1	2				
7			10			
14			17	18	19	
	22				26	27
28	29	30	31			

1. Color the day after August 14 red.
2. Color the day before August 27 green.
3. Color the third Wednesday yellow.

173

Money

Match the coins with the values.

① Dime •

② Quarter •

③ Nickel •

④ Penny •

• 25¢

• 10¢

• 1¢

• 5¢

¢
means cent.

Cross out ✗ the coins you count and write the numbers.

⑤ Number of pennies : ☐

⑥ Number of nickels : ☐

⑦ Number of dimes : ☐

⑧ Number of quarters : ☐

How much is each coin worth? Check ✔ the right answer.

⑨
A more than 20¢
B less than 20¢

⑩
A more than 20¢
B less than 20¢

⑪
A more than 20¢
B less than 20¢

⑫
A more than 20¢
B less than 20¢

174

Check ✔ the coins to match the value of the coin on the left.

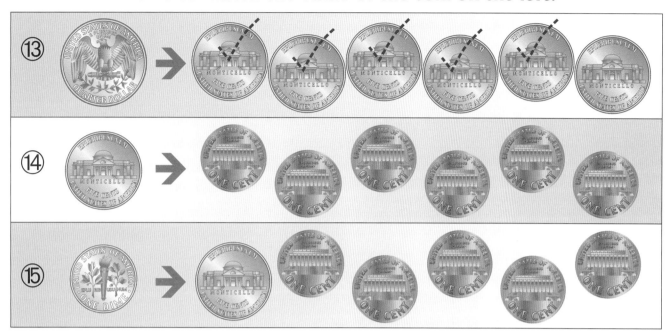

Write how much each child has.

⑯ ☐ ¢

⑰ ☐ ¢

⑱ ☐ ¢

⑲ ☐ ¢

⑳ Circle the child who has the most money.

1 quarter	=	25¢
1 dime	=	10¢
1 nickel	=	5¢
1 penny	=	1¢

Check ✔ the coins needed to buy each item.

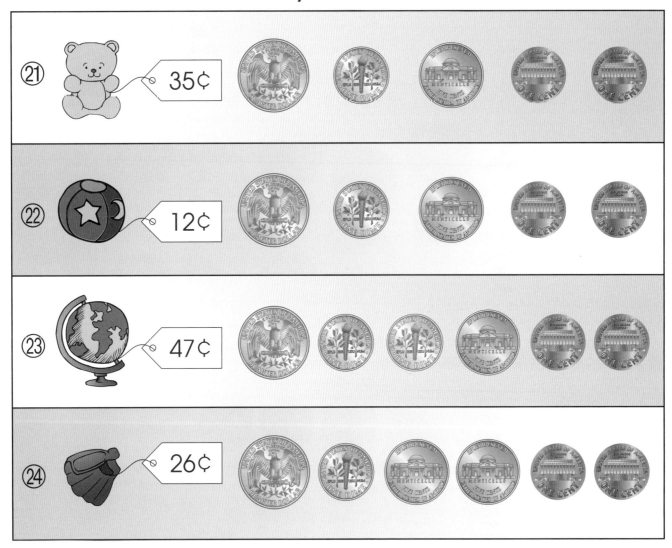

Pay with the fewest coins. Write the number of coins.

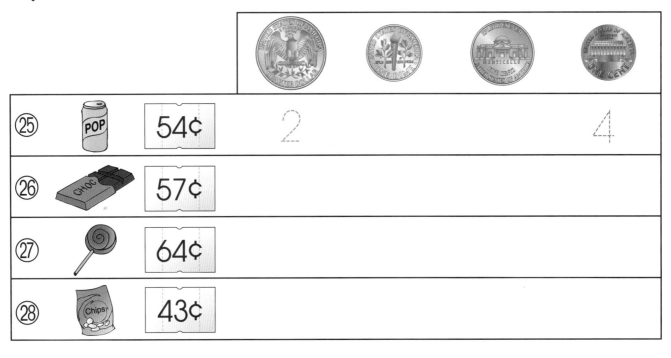

How much did each child spend? How much does each child have now?

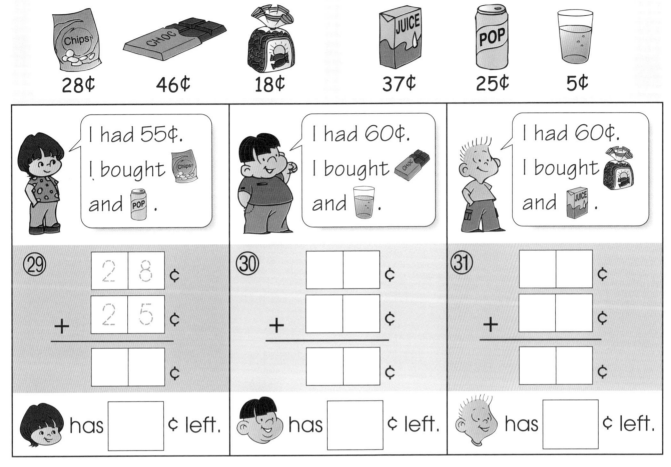

LOW PRICE STORE

Snacks

Chips 28¢   CHOC 46¢   18¢

Drinks

JUICE 37¢   POP 25¢   5¢

I had 55¢. I bought Chips and POP.

㉙
```
   2  8  ¢
+  2  5  ¢
         ¢
```
has ☐ ¢ left.

I had 60¢. I bought CHOC and ☐.

㉚
```
      ¢
+     ¢
      ¢
```
has ☐ ¢ left.

I had 60¢. I bought and JUICE.

㉛
```
      ¢
+     ¢
      ¢
```
has ☐ ¢ left.

ACTIVITY

Jill and Mark share the coins equally. How many coins does each get? How much does each get?

1. Each has ☐ coins.

2. Each has ☐ ¢.

Look at the shapes. Then check ✔ the right sentences.

①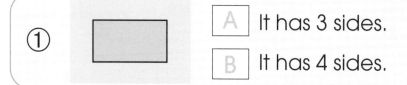
- A It has 3 sides.
- B It has 4 sides.

②
- A It has 1 right angle.
- B It has no angles.

③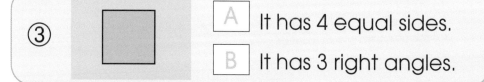
- A It has 4 equal sides.
- B It has 3 right angles.

④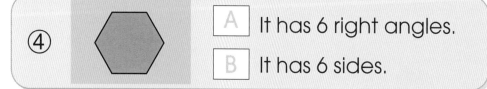
- A It has 6 right angles.
- B It has 6 sides.

⑤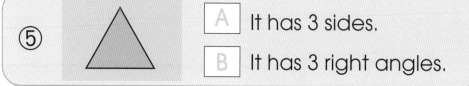
- A It has 3 sides.
- B It has 3 right angles.

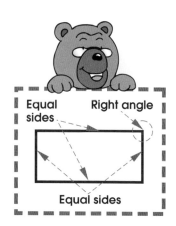

Equal sides   Right angle

Equal sides

Count and write the number of shapes.

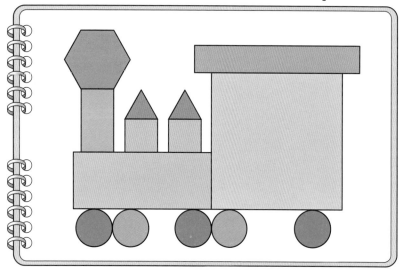

⑥ Rectangle

⑦ Triangle

⑧ Circle

⑨ Square

⑩ Hexagon

Two sides of my face match exactly. It has symmetry.

A shape having symmetry means it has both sides matching exactly.

Do these shapes have symmetry? Circle Yes or No.

⑪  Yes   No

⑫ 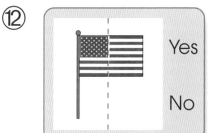 Yes   No

⑬  Yes   No

⑭  Yes   No

⑮ 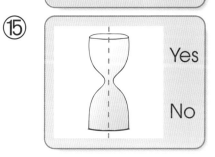 Yes   No

⑯ 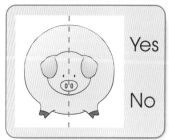 Yes   No

Draw a line to cut each shape into two matching parts.

⑰

⑱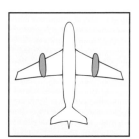

⑲

⑳

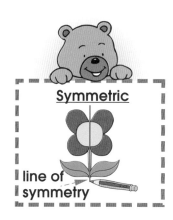

Symmetric

line of symmetry

㉑

㉒

㉓

Draw the matching part of each shape from the dotted line. Write the name of the completed shape in the ☐ **.**

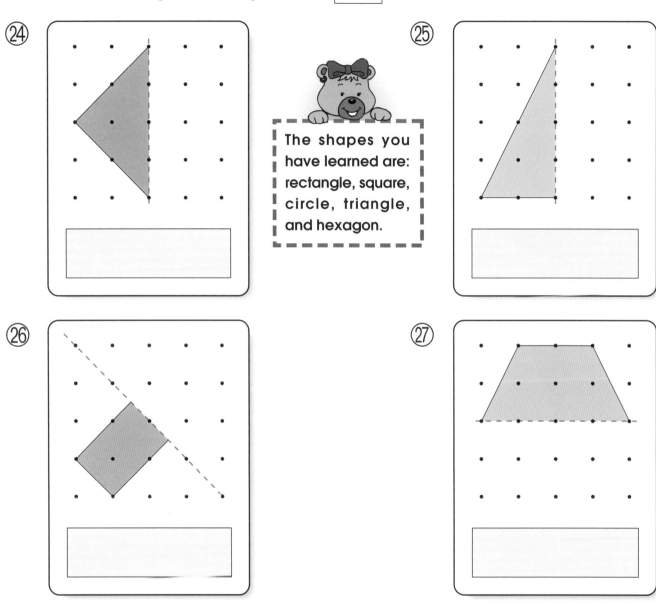

The shapes you have learned are: rectangle, square, circle, triangle, and hexagon.

Draw a line to cut each shape in half and color half of it.

Jill has made a shape with a tangram. Write the numbers in the **.**

This is a tangram. It has seven pieces.

㉜

A kitten

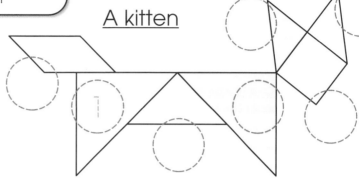

ACTIVITY

1. How many triangles are there ?

     triangles

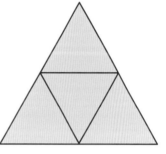

2. On each shape, draw as many lines as you can to cut the shape into matching parts.

    a.

    b.

3. Check ✔ the shape formed with a tangram.

    a.

    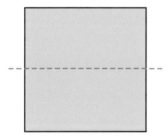

    b.

    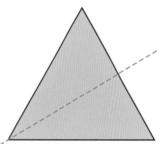

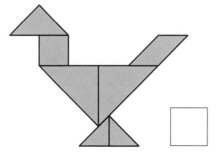

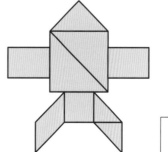

13 *Pictographs*

Count the pets and write the numbers.

The Pets We Have

🐱			
🐱			
🐱	🐶		
🐱	🐶		
🐱	🐶	🐦	
🐱	🐶	🐦	🐭
🐱	🐶	🐦	🐭
🐱	🐶	🐦	🐭

① There are ☐ 🐱 .

② There are ☐ 🐶 .

③ There are ☐ 🐦 .

④ There arc ☐ 🐭 .

⑤ There are ☐ more 🐱 than 🐶 .

⑥ There are ☐ more 🐶 than 🐭 .

⑦ There are ☐ pets in all.

Look at the pictograph and circle the right answers.

Here are the favorite foods of my class.

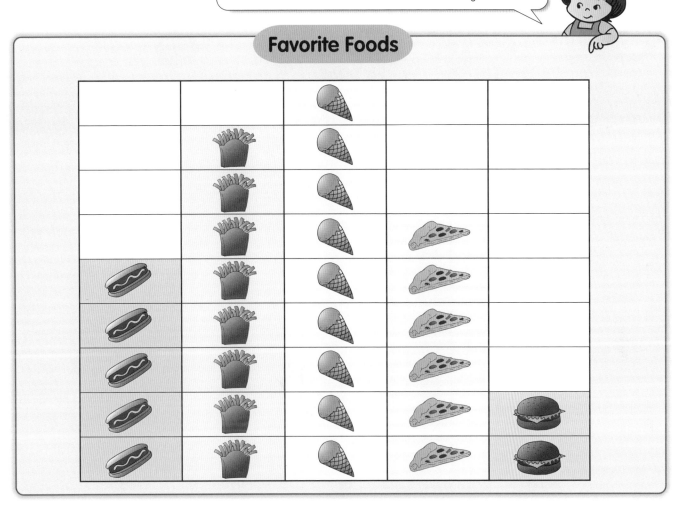

Favorite Foods

⑧ How many students like   ?   5   7   9

⑨ 8 students like   .

⑩ Most students like   .

⑪ Fewest students like   .

⑫ How many students like or ?   15   16   17

⑬ How many students are there?   25   30   35

Read what Jill says. Make a graph and fill in the blanks.

I have 5 🎎 , 3 🚗 , 6 🐕 , and 5 ⚽ .

⑭ Color the ☐ to complete the graph.

Jill's Toys

⑮ There is ☐ more 🐕 than 🎎 .

⑯ There are ☐ more 🎎 than 🚗 .

⑰ There are ☐ 🎎 and ⚽ in all.

⑱ There are ☐ 🐕 and ⚽ in all.

⑲ There are ☐ toys in all.

Sort Jill's cards and circle the right answers.

⑳ Color the ☐ to complete the graph.

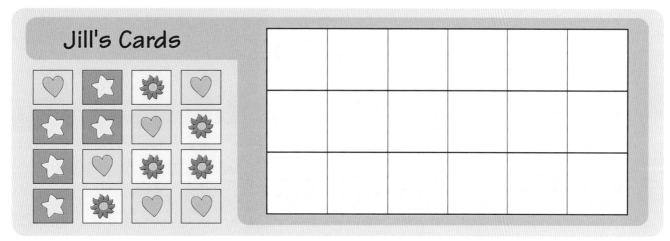

Jill's Cards

㉑ How many ♡ are there?   5   6   7

㉒ How many 🌻 are there?   5   6   7

㉓ Jill has the most ♡   ⭐   🌻 .

㉔ She has   15   16   17   cards in all.

ACTIVITY

Answer the questions.

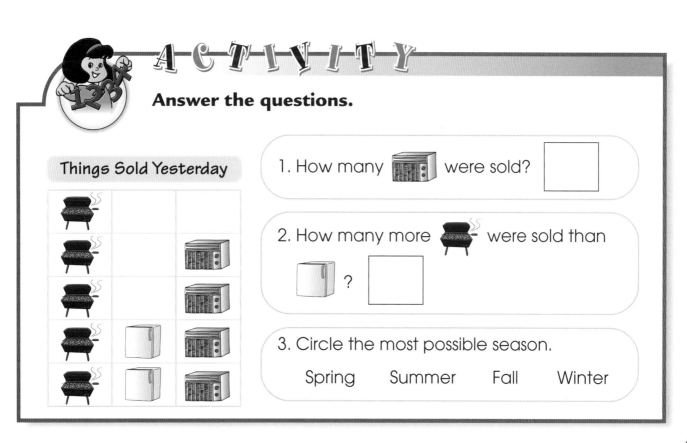

Things Sold Yesterday

1. How many [air conditioner] were sold? ☐

2. How many more [grill] were sold than [air conditioner] ? ☐

3. Circle the most possible season.

   Spring   Summer   Fall   Winter

Write the numbers. (28 marks)

①
4	8
3	9

+

②
5	2
1	1

−

③
	4
3	7

+

④
4	6
3	6

+

⑤
8	8
5	5

−

⑥
9	3
3	3

−

⑦ 25 + 16 = ☐

⑧ 3 + 19 = ☐

⑨ 23 + 57 = ☐

⑩ 48 − 17 = ☐

⑪ 62 − 62 = ☐

⑫ 79 − 59 = ☐

⑬ 14 + 23 + 11 = ☐

⑭ 59 + 11 + 6 = ☐

Read the points that the children got in the game. Do questions 15-19.
(10 marks)

	1st ball	2nd ball	3rd ball
	39	0	25
	16	20	40
	43	28	0

⑮ How many points did get?

$\boxed{} + \boxed{} + \boxed{} = \boxed{}$

 got $\boxed{}$ points.

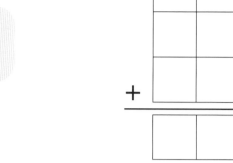

⑯ How many points did 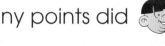 get?

$\boxed{} + \boxed{} + \boxed{} = \boxed{}$

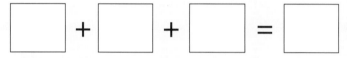 got $\boxed{}$ points.

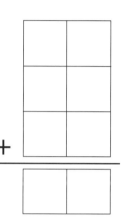

⑰ How many points did get?

$\boxed{} + \boxed{} + \boxed{} = \boxed{}$

 got $\boxed{}$ points.

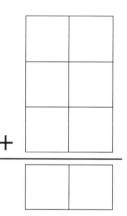

⑱ How many more points did get than ?

$\boxed{} - \boxed{} = \boxed{}$

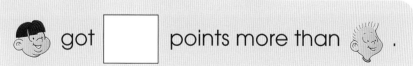 got $\boxed{}$ points more than .

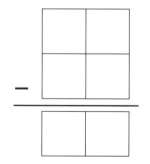

⑲ Circle the child with the highest points.

Match the words with the right pictures. (8 marks)

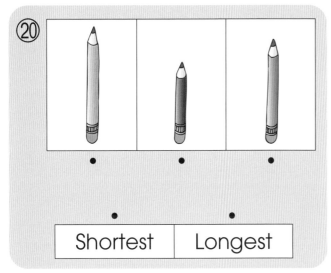

Shortest | Longest

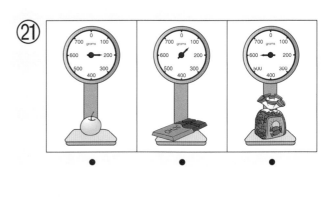

Heaviest | Lightest

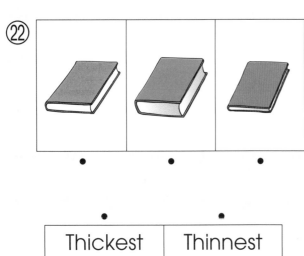

Thickest | Thinnest

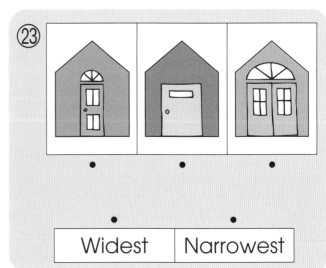

Widest | Narrowest

Use a ruler to measure the box. Write the numbers. (4 marks)

24 Length = ☐ in

25 Width = ☐ in

26 Height = ☐ in

27 How many ☐ on the

lid? ☐ ☐

Write the times or draw the clock hands. (10 marks)

 28 [ ] o'clock

 29 half past [ ]

 30 half past 9

 32 [ ] o'clock

 31 half past [ ]

Write the days and months. (5 marks)

33 Sunday → _____ → _____ →

Wednesday → _____ → Friday → Saturday

34 May → _____ → _____ → August

Match the seasons with the temperatures. Put a check mark ✔ in the right [ ]. (4 marks)

Season \ Weather	Warmest	Coldest	Getting warmer	Getting colder
35 Spring				
36 Summer				
37 Fall				
38 Winter				

Write how much money each child has and tell who has more money.
(6 marks)

(41) Circle the child who has more money.

Pay with the fewest coins. Write the numbers. (4 marks)

(42) 🚗 35¢				
(43) 40¢				
(44) 26¢				
(45) 48¢				

Draw a line to cut each shape into two matching parts. (3 marks)

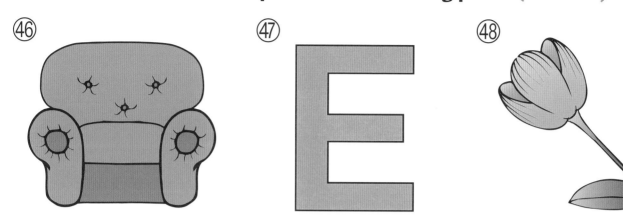

㊻ ㊼ ㊽

Draw the matching parts of each shape from the dotted line. (4 marks)

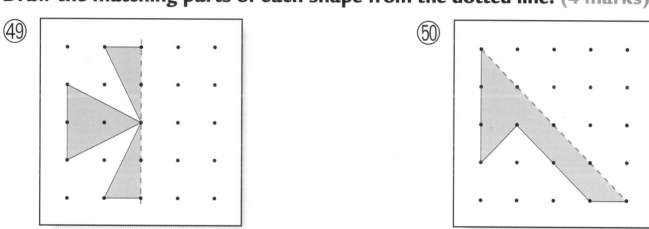

㊾ ㊿

Show how many 🍬 the children got in the game. (6 marks)

Number of 🍬	4	8	9

�51 Color the 🍬 to complete the graph.

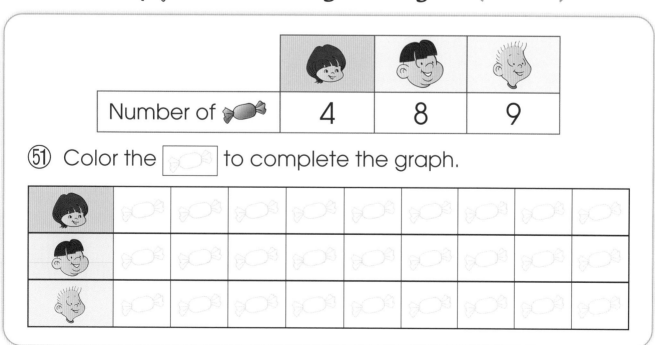

Look at Jill's pictograph and answer the questions. (8 marks)

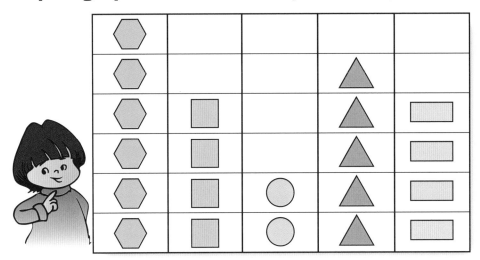

㊽ Write the numbers.

a. Jill has ☐ hexagons.

b. Jill has ☐ squares.

c. Jill has ☐ more triangles than circles.

d. Jill has ☐ hexagons and circles in all.

㊾ Circle the right answers.

a. Jill has the most hexagons   triangles   rectangles .

b. Jill has the fewest rectangles   squares   circles .

c. Jill has the same number of squares

hexagons , and triangles   rectangles .

SCORE
100

Section IV

Overview

In Section III, children were introduced to the five major areas of mathematics: Number Sense and Numeration, Measurement, Geometry and Spatial Sense, Patterning and Algebra, and Data Management and Probability.

In this section, concepts of shape, money, measurement, graph, addition and subtraction are further developed and practiced in integrated exercises.

Solving "story problems" provides children with practice in reading as well as translating words into mathematical terms. The exercises describe everyday situations to provide context and interest for the Grade 1 students.

Numbers 1 to 10

Use the pictures to answer the questions.

 Helen's basket

 Barry's basket

① How many 🍎 are there in Helen's basket? _____ 🍎

② How many 🍎 are there in Barry's basket? _____ 🍎

③ Who has more 🍎 ? _____

Dan's tower   Rick's tower   Eva's tower

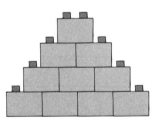 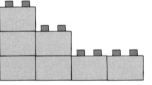

④ How many 🧱 are there in Dan's tower? _____ 🧱

⑤ How many 🧱 are there in Rick's tower? _____ 🧱

⑥ How many 🧱 are there in Eva's tower? _____ 🧱

⑦ Who has the most 🧱 ? _____

⑧ Who has the fewest 🧱 ? _____

⑨ If Eva puts 1 more 🧱 on her tower, how many

🧱 are there in her new tower?  _____ 🧱

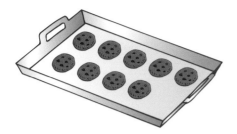		
Jamie's cookies	Carmen's cookies	Lucy's cookies

⑩ How many 🍪 does Jamie have? _____ 🍪

⑪ How many 🍪 does Carmen have? _____ 🍪

⑫ How many 🍪 does Lucy have? _____ 🍪

⑬ How many 🍪 could Jamie give to his friends if he ate one himself? _____ 🍪

⑭ How many 🍪 would Lucy have if she got one from Jamie? _____ 🍪

Fill in the blanks.

⑮ How many boys are there? _____ boys

⑯ How many girls are there? _____ girls

⑰ How many children are there? _____ children

⑱ Who is the 1st in the line? _____

⑲ Who is the 3rd in the line? _____

Addition and Subtraction to 10

See how many stickers each child has. Answer the questions.

① Ann has _____ ☺ .

② Bobby has _____ ☺ .

③ Carol has _____ ☺ .

④ Deb has _____ ☺ .

⑤ _____ has the most ☺ ; _____ has the fewest ☺ .

⑥ Ann and Bobby have _____ ☺ in all.

⑦ Bobby and Deb have _____ ☺ in all.

⑧ Ann and Deb have _____ ☺ in all.

⑨ Ann has _____ fewer ☺ than Carol.

⑩ Carol has _____ more ☺ than Bobby.

⑪ Carol has _____ more ☺ than Deb.

Use the pictures to answer the questions.

⑫ How many 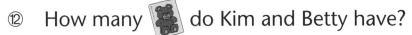 do Kim and Betty have? _____

⑬ How many more 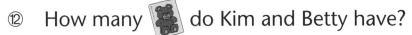 does Kim have than Betty? _____

⑭ Kim gives 1 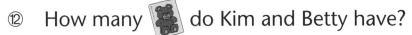 to Betty, how many 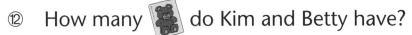 does he have now? _____

⑮ How many 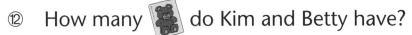 does Betty have now? _____

⑯ How many are there in all? _____

⑰ How many more are there on the plate than in the box? _____

⑱ There are 4 chocolate on the plate. How many on the plate are not chocolate flavored? _____

⑲ Joey puts 3 more on the plate. How many are on the plate now? _____

⑳ Julia takes 2 from the box. How many are left? _____

See how many biscuits each child ate yesterday. Then answer the questions.

	Brian	Dave	Beth
Morning	2 biscuits	3 biscuits	5 biscuits
Afternoon	4 biscuits	7 biscuits	2 biscuits

㉑ How many 🍪 did Brian eat in all?   _____ 🍪

㉒ How many 🍪 did Dave eat in all?   _____ 🍪

㉓ How many 🍪 did Beth eat in all?   _____ 🍪

㉔ How many 🍪 did the children eat in the morning?   _____ 🍪

㉕ How many more 🍪 did Brian eat in the afternoon than in the morning?   _____ 🍪

㉖ How many fewer 🍪 did Dave eat in the morning than in the afternoon?   _____ 🍪

㉗ How many fewer 🍪 did Beth eat in the afternoon than in the morning?   _____ 🍪

㉘ If Beth ate 3 more 🍪 in the afternoon, how many 🍪 did he eat the whole day?   _____ 🍪

See what Jack has for his birthday party. Then write the numbers.

㉙ There are _____ 🎈 and _____ 🎈 .

㉚ If 2 🎈 burst, _____ 🎈 are left.

㉛ Jack's mom buys 6 🍾 . _____ 🍾 are not on the table.

㉜ Jack fills 3 🥤 with pop. _____ 🥤 are not filled.

㉝ Jack is 7 years old. He needs to put _____ more 🕯 on the cake.

㉞ 4 boys and 3 girls come to the party. _____ children come to the party in all.

㉟ Each guest takes 1 🎉 . _____ 🎉 are left.

㊱ Each girl takes 1 🍴 . _____ 🍴 are left.

㊲ There are 10 🍽 on the table. If each girl takes 1 🍽 , _____ 🍽 are left.

Addition and Subtraction to 20

See how many candies each child collected at Halloween. Count and write the numbers. Then answer the questions.

①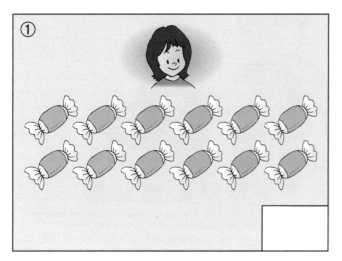

②

③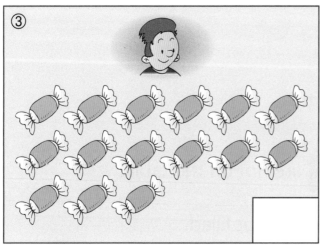

④

⑤ ate 5 . How many are left? _____

⑥ ate 3 . How many are left? _____

⑦ gave 2 to . How many

are left? _____

⑧ How many does have now? _____

200

Look at the fruits Brad's mom bought. Count and write the numbers. Then answer the questions.

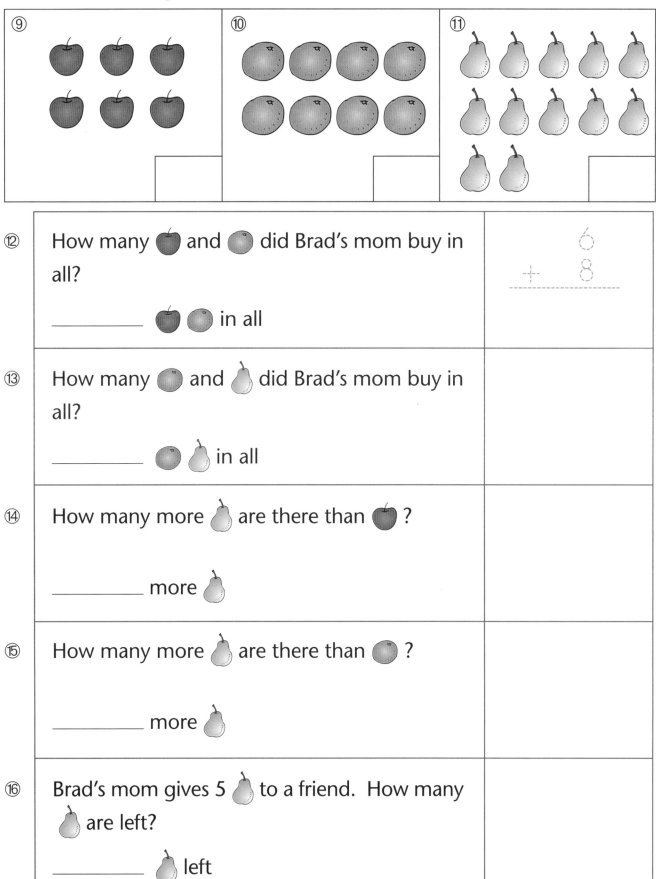

⑨

⑩

⑪

⑫ How many 🍎 and 🍊 did Brad's mom buy in all?

_____ 🍎 🍊 in all

$$\begin{array}{r} 6 \\ + \; 8 \\ \hline \end{array}$$

⑬ How many 🍊 and 🍐 did Brad's mom buy in all?

_____ 🍊 🍐 in all

⑭ How many more 🍐 are there than 🍎 ?

_____ more 🍐

⑮ How many more 🍐 are there than 🍊 ?

_____ more 🍐

⑯ Brad's mom gives 5 🍐 to a friend. How many 🍐 are left?

_____ 🍐 left

Answer the questions.

⑰ Ann has 7 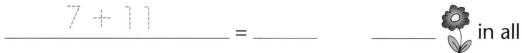; Grace has 11 . How many do they have in all?

_____7 + 11_____ = _____   _____ in all

⑱ How many more does Grace have than Ann?

_____ = _____   _____ more

⑲ In Mrs. Ling's class, there are 17 . 5 are . How many are there?

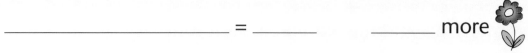

_____ = _____   _____

⑳ How many more are there than ?

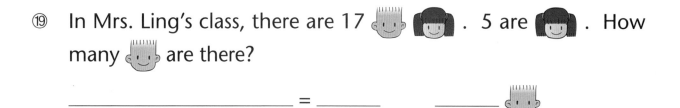

_____ = _____   _____ more

㉑ Tim has 13 ; Rick has 7 . How many do they have in all?

_____ = _____   _____ in all

㉒ How many more does Tim have than Rick?

_____ = _____   _____ more

㉓ Mrs. White buys 3 🍩 . Mrs. Wenn buys 11 🍩 . How many
🍩 do they buy in all?

_____ = _____   _____ 🍩 in all

㉔ How many more 🍩 does Mrs. Wenn buy than Mrs. White?

_____ = _____   _____ more 🍩

㉕ Mr. Stanley has 3 🛍 of 🍎 . Each 🛍 has 6 🍎 . How many
🍎 are there in all?

_____ = _____   _____ 🍎 in all

㉖ If Mr. Stanley wants to have 20 🍎 , how many more 🍎 does he
need to buy?

_____ = _____   _____ more 🍎

㉗ Ben is 12 years old. How old was he 4 years ago?

_____ = _____   _____ years old

㉘ How old will he be after 5 years?

_____ = _____   _____ years old

203

Shapes

Write 'cone', 'cylinder', 'prism', or 'sphere' in the boxes. Then match similar shapes.

①

Mandy gets 4 boxes of chocolates for Valentine's Day. Write 'cube', 'cylinder', 'prism', or 'pyramid' in the boxes. Then put a check mark ✔ in the circle for the one that can roll.

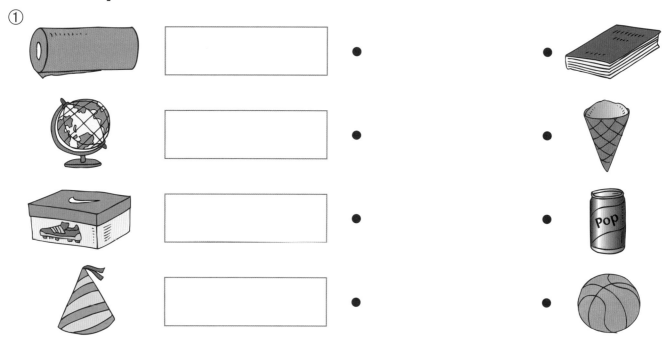

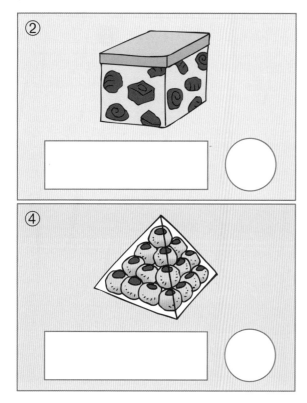

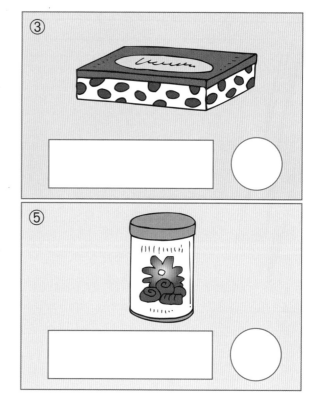

Check ✔ the correct sentences and cross out ✗ the wrong ones.

⑥   A prism can slide.   ◯

⑦   A cylinder can slide and roll.   ◯

⑧   A sphere can roll but not slide.   ◯

⑨   A cube can roll and slide.   ◯

⑩   A pyramid can roll.   ◯

See how many blocks are needed to build each tower. Then answer the questions.

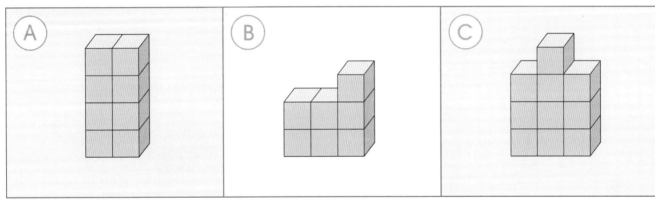

⑪   How many blocks are needed to build tower A?   _____ blocks

⑫   How many blocks are needed to build tower B?   _____ blocks

⑬   How many blocks are needed to build tower C?   _____ blocks

⑭   Which of the towers is a prism?   Tower _____

⑮   What is the fewest number of blocks you need to
     add on tower B to make it a prism?   _____

Look at the colored part of each flag. Then name the shape.

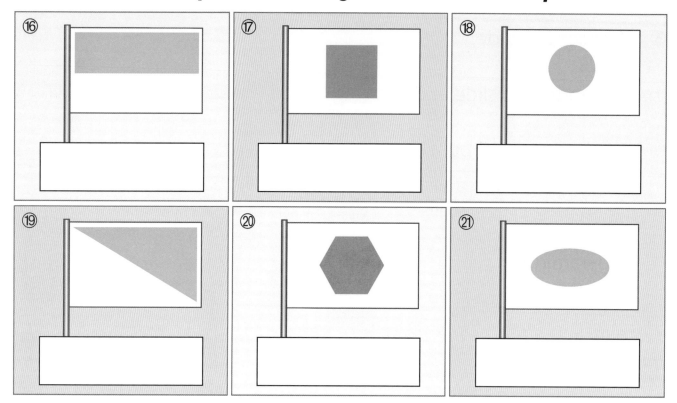

Look at the shapes and complete the table.

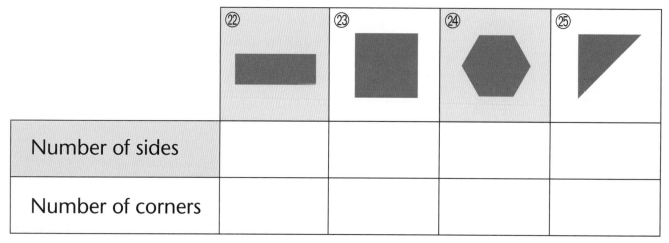

	⑳	㉓	㉔	㉕
Number of sides				
Number of corners				

Draw a line to cut each shape into two matching parts.

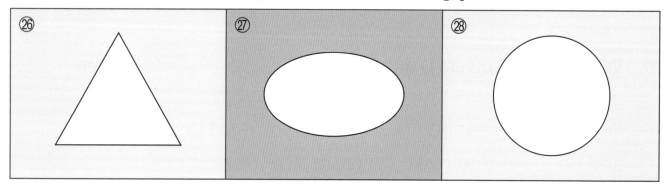

Draw the matching part of each shape from the dotted line.

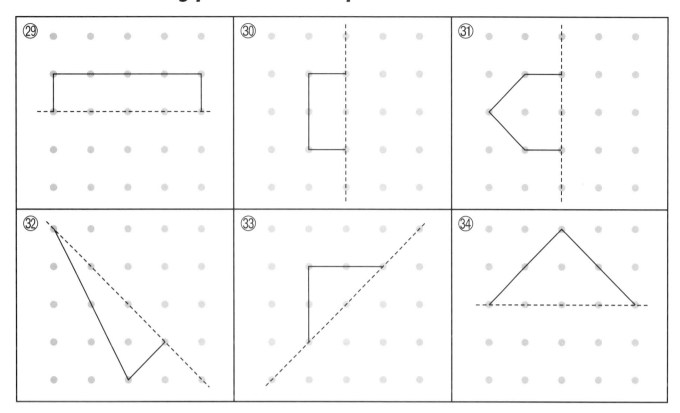

See how many books Uncle Bill uses to cover each board. Estimate and count. Write the numbers.

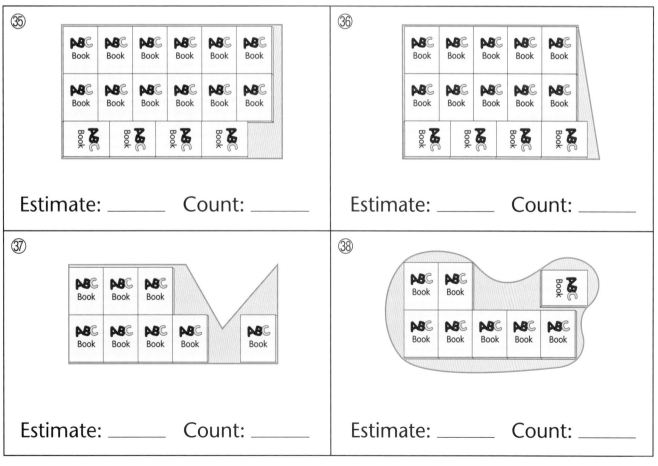

③⑤ Estimate: _____ Count: _____

③⑥ Estimate: _____ Count: _____

③⑦ Estimate: _____ Count: _____

③⑧ Estimate: _____ Count: _____

Solid Column Graphs

The graph shows which sports the students like best. Check ✔ the correct answers.

① Which is the most popular sport?

 A   B   C

② Which is the least popular sport?

 A   B   C

③ How many students like best?

Ⓐ 3   Ⓑ 4   Ⓒ 5

④ How many more students like than ?

Ⓐ 1   Ⓑ 2   Ⓒ 3

⑤ How many students are asked?

Ⓐ 12   Ⓑ 13   Ⓒ 14

Kay, Kim, and Karen are collecting stickers. See how many stickers they have and answer the questions.

⑥ Who has the most ⭐ ?   _____

⑦ Who has the fewest ⭐ ?   _____

⑧ How many ⭐ does Kay have?   _____ ⭐

⑨ How many ⭐ does Kim have?   _____ ⭐

⑩ How many ⭐ does Karen have?   _____ ⭐

⑪ How many ⭐ do Kay and Kim have?   _____ ⭐

⑫ How many more ⭐ does Karen have than
    Kim?   _____ ⭐

⑬ How many ⭐ do they have in all?   _____ ⭐

⑭ If Kay collects 5 more ⭐ , how many does
    he have in all?   _____ ⭐

Count the fishes in the tank. Then answer the questions and color the pictures to complete the graph.

⑮ How many  are there?   _____

⑯ How many  are there?   _____

⑰ How many  are there?   _____

⑱ How many  are there?   _____

Fishes in the Tank

⑲

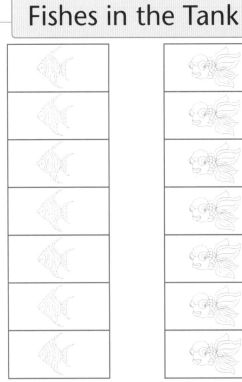  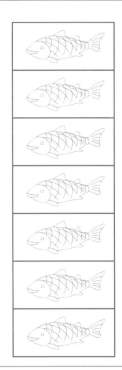

Count the animals in the pet shop. Then answer the questions and color the pictures to complete the graph.

20. How many types of animals are there? _____ types

21. How many birds are there? _____ birds

22. How many rabbits are there? _____ rabbits

23. How many dogs are there? _____ dogs

24. How many cats are there? _____ cats

25.

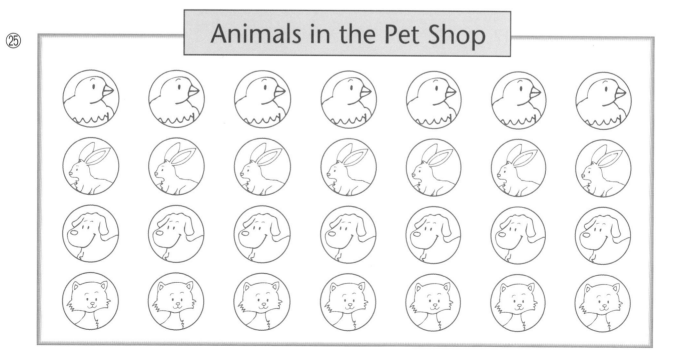

Count the ice cubes each child has. Then answer the questions.

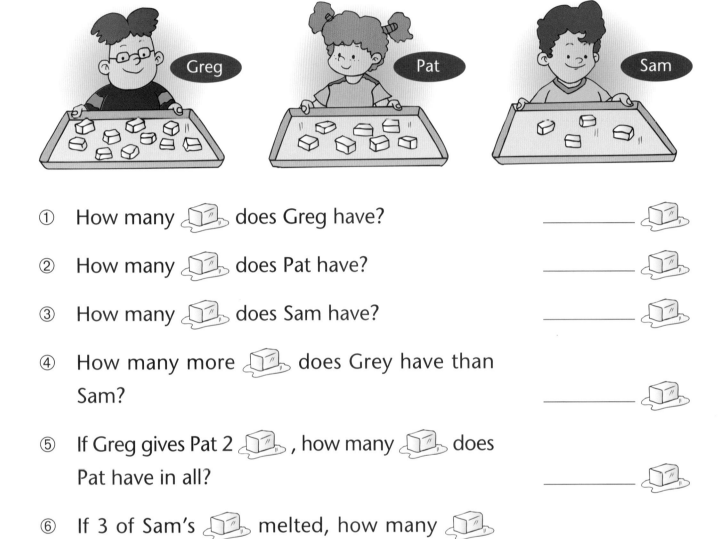

① How many does Greg have? _____

② How many does Pat have? _____

③ How many does Sam have? _____

④ How many more does Grey have than Sam? _____

⑤ If Greg gives Pat 2 , how many does Pat have in all? _____

⑥ If 3 of Sam's melted, how many would be left? _____

Color the things which have the shape of a sphere.

⑦

The pictures show how many glasses of milk the children drink in a week. Use the pictures to answer the questions.

Sue	Mabel	Paul	Sam

⑧ Sue drinks _____  in a week.

⑨ Mabel drinks _____  in a week.

⑩ Paul drinks _____  in a week.

⑪ Sam drinks _____  in a week.

⑫ Sue and Paul drink _____ 🥛 in all.

⑬ Mabel and Sam drink _____ 🥛 in all.

⑭ Mabel drinks _____ more 🥛 than Paul.

⑮ The girls drink _____ 🥛 in all.

⑯ The boys drink _____ 🥛 in all.

⑰ The boys drink _____ 🥛 fewer than the girls.

⑱ If Paul drinks 7 more 🥛 , he will drink _____ 🥛 in a week.

213

Look at the shapes of Judy's containers. Check ✔ the correct answers and color the pictures to complete the graph.

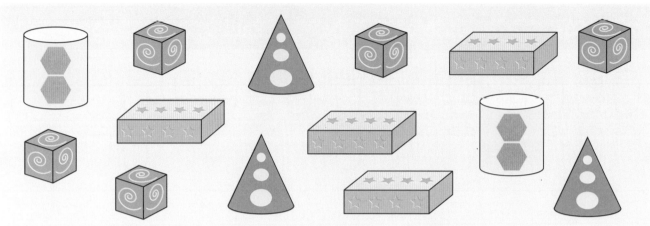

⑲ How many types of shapes are in Judy's collection?

(A) 2   (B) 3   (C) 4

⑳ Which shape does Judy have the most?

(A) cylinder   (B) cube   (C) prism

㉑ How many cones does Judy have?

(A) 2   (B) 3   (C) 4

㉒ How many cubes and cylinders does Judy have in all?

(A) 6   (B) 7   (C) 8

㉓ How many more cubes are there than cones?

(A) 2   (B) 3   (C) 4

㉔ How many containers does Judy have in all?

(A) 12   (B) 13   (C) 14

㉕

Judy's Collection

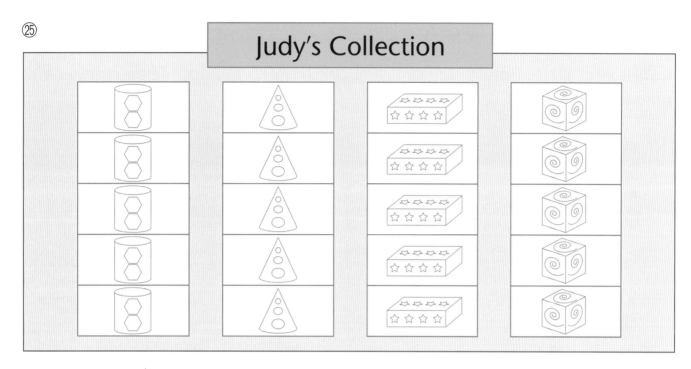

Lucy traces the shapes on the paper. Match the containers with the shapes and write the names of the shapes.

㉖

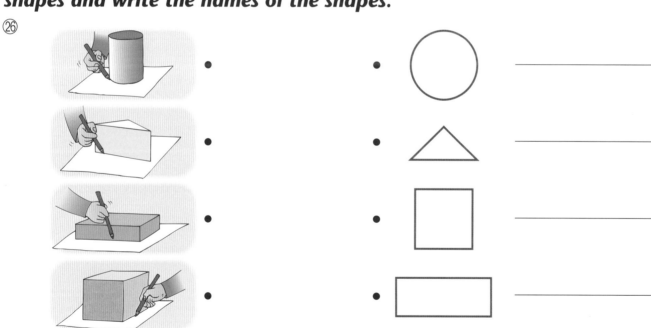

Draw a line to cut each shape into two matching parts.

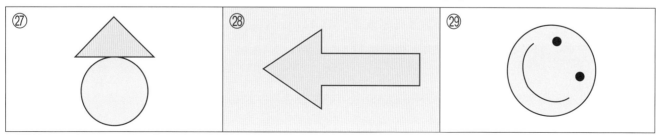

Numbers 20 to 100

Count and write how many crayons are in each group. Then answer the questions.

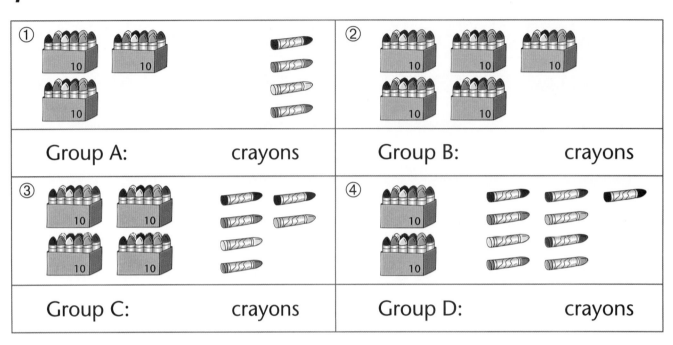

Group A: _____ crayons

Group B: _____ crayons

Group C: _____ crayons

Group D: _____ crayons

⑤ Which group has the most crayons ? Group _____

⑥ Which group has the fewest crayons ? Group _____

⑦ Put the groups in order from the one that has the most crayons to the one that has the fewest.

Group _____ , Group _____ , Group _____ , Group _____

⑧ If Wayne puts 10 more crayons in Group B, how many crayons are there in all? _____ crayons

⑨ If George takes 10 crayons away from Group C, how many crayons will be left? _____ crayons

⑩ Jill has 1 crayon more than Group D. How many crayons does she have? _____ crayons

The children put the pennies in piles of 10. Write how many pennies each child has. Then answer the questions.

⑪

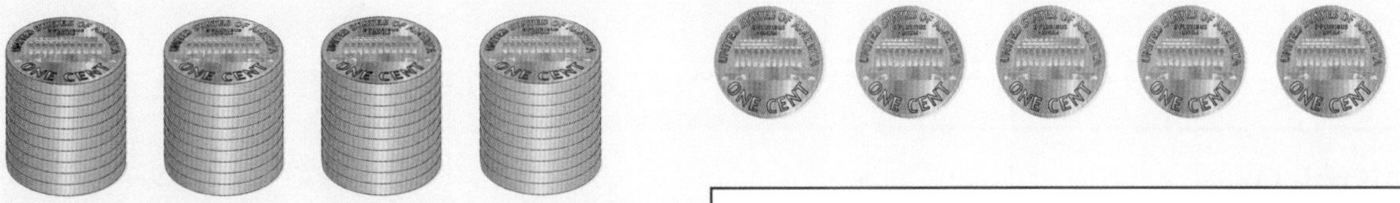

Lily has ________ .

⑫

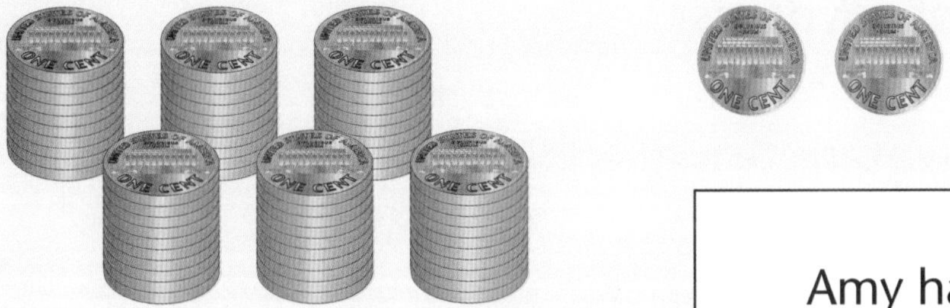

Amy has ________ .

⑬

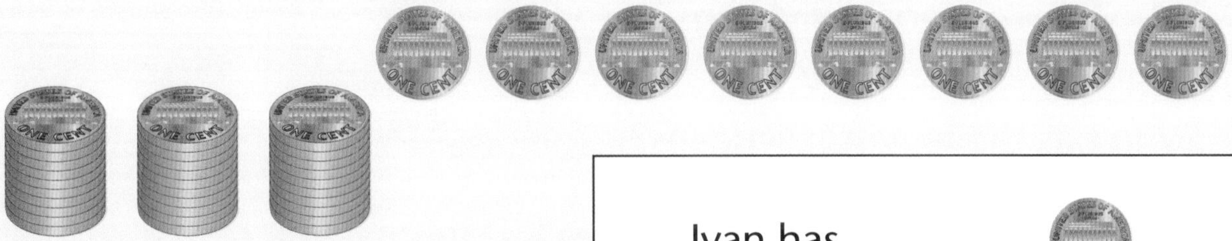

Ivan has ________ .

⑭ ________ has the most money.

⑮ ________ has the least money.

⑯ Put the children in order from the one who has the most money to the one who has the least.

________ , ________ , ________

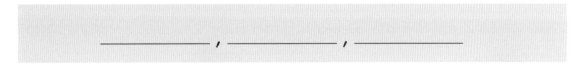

⑰ Ivan gives 1 pile of to Lily. Ivan has ________ left.

⑱ Amy gets 5 more . She has ________ in all.

See how many jellybeans each child has. Use the table to answer the questions.

	Brenda	Derek	Mike	Dan
Number of jellybeans	79	52	69	78

⑲ Who has seventy-eight jellybeans? _____

⑳ Who has 10 fewer jellybeans than Brenda? _____

㉑ Who has 1 more jellybean than Dan? _____

㉒ Who has the most jellybeans? _____

㉓ Who has the fewest jellybeans? _____

㉔ Put the children in order from the one who has the fewest jellybeans to the one who has the most.

_____ , _____ , _____ , _____

㉕ Mike gives 1 jellybean to Derek. Mike has _____ jellybeans left and Derek has _____ jelly beans in all.

㉖ Brenda gives 2 jellybeans to Dan. Dan has _____ jellybeans in all and Brenda has _____ jellybeans left.

㉗ _____ has the most jellybeans now.

Read what the children say. Then write the numbers on the fence.

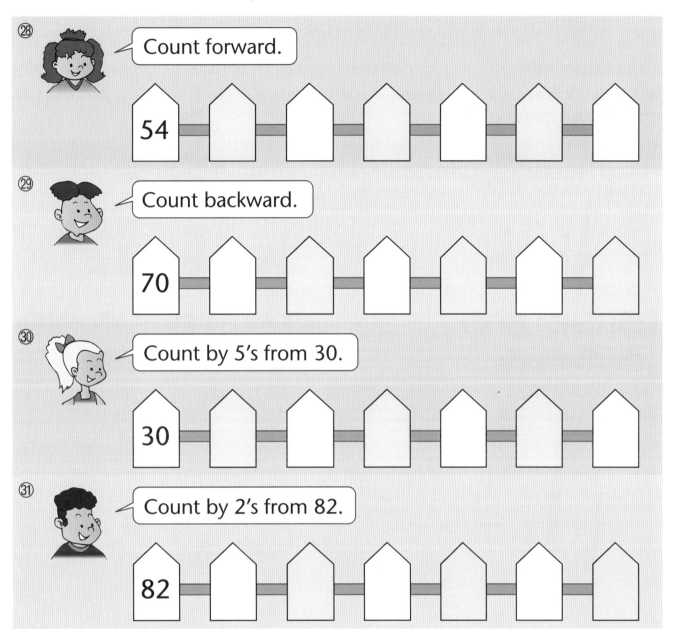

28 Count forward.

54

29 Count backward.

70

30 Count by 5's from 30.

30

31 Count by 2's from 82.

82

Answer the questions.

32 Jim has 68 ⊙ ; Mary has 72 ⊙ . Who has
more ⊙ ?   _____

33 William has 48 🍭 ; Stephen has 51 🍭 . Who
has fewer 🍭 ?   _____

34 Alvin has 25 🍬 ; Louis has 20 more 🍬 than
Alvin. How many 🍬 does Louis have?   _____ 🍬

7 Addition and Subtraction to 50

Calculators may be used to calculate or check answers. Count and write how many boys and girls are in each group. Then use the pictures to answer the questions.

① Group A	② Group B

③ How many boys are there in all?

_____ = _____   _____ boys

④ How many girls are there in all?

_____ = _____   _____ girls

⑤ How many children are in Group A?

_____ = _____   _____ children

⑥ How many children are in Group B?

_____ = _____   _____ children

⑦ How many children are there in all?

_____ = _____   _____ children

See how many pins are in each pincushion. Use the pictures to answer the questions.

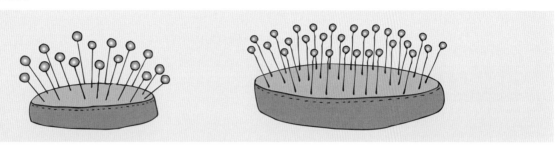

⑧ How many 📍 are in the small pincushion? _____ 📍

⑨ How many 📍 are in the big pincushion? _____ 📍

⑩ How many 📍 are there in all?

_____ = _____   _____ 📍

⑪ How many more 📍 are in the big pincushion than in the small one?

_____ = _____   _____ 📍

⑫ If Mrs. Smith puts 15 more 📍 in the small pincushion, how many 📍 are there in the small pincushion?

_____ = _____   _____ 📍

⑬ If Aunt Molly puts 15 more 📍 in the big pincushion, how many 📍 are there in the big pincushion?

_____ = _____   _____ 📍

⑭ If Lucy takes out 16 📍 from the big pincushion, how many 📍 are left in the big pincushion?

_____ = _____   _____ 📍

Brenda, Mike, and Dan collected some shells on Monday and Tuesday. Look at the record and answer the questions.

	Monday	Tuesday
Brenda	15	17
Mike	11	14
Dan	18	19

⑮ How many 🐚 did Brenda collect in all?

_____ = _____   _____ 🐚

⑯ How many 🐚 did Mike collect in all?

_____ = _____   _____ 🐚

⑰ How many 🐚 did Dan collect in all?

_____ = _____   _____ 🐚

⑱ How many more 🐚 did Dan collect than Mike?

_____ = _____   _____ 🐚

⑲ How many 🐚 did the children collect on Monday?

_____ = _____   _____ 🐚

⑳ How many 🐚 did the children collect on Tuesday?

_____ = _____   _____ 🐚

Look at the record showing the loaves of bread baked and sold in the past 3 days. Then answer the questions.

	Thursday	Friday	Saturday
Number of 🍞 baked	21	24	28
Number of 🍞 sold	17	18	19

㉑ How many 🍞 were left on Thursday?

_____ = _____   _____

㉒ How many 🍞 were left on Friday?

_____ = _____   _____

㉓ How many 🍞 were left on Saturday?

_____ = _____   _____

㉔ How many 🍞 did the baker bake on Thursday and Friday?

_____ = _____   _____

㉕ How many 🍞 did the baker bake on Thursday and Saturday?

_____ = _____   _____

㉖ How many 🍞 were sold on Friday and Saturday?

_____ = _____   _____

Addition and Subtraction to 100

Calculators can be used to calculate or check answers. Count and write how many shells each child collected. Then answer the questions.

① Peter

② Roger

③ Tina

④ How many 🐚 did Peter and Tina collect in all?

[ ] + [ ] = [ ]

They collected [ ] 🐚 in all.

[ ]
+ [ ]
―――
[ ]

⑤ How many more 🐚 did Tina collect than Roger?

[ ] – [ ] = [ ]

Tina collected [ ] more 🐚 than Roger.

[ ]
– [ ]
―――
[ ]

⑥ How many 🐚 did the boys collect in all?

[   ] + [   ] = [   ]

They collected [   ] 🐚 in all.

+ [   ]
  [   ]
  ———
  [   ]

⑦ How many more 🐚 did Peter collect than Roger?

[   ] – [   ] = [   ]

Peter collected [   ] more 🐚 than Roger.

– [   ]
  [   ]
  ———
  [   ]

⑧ Tina's goal was to collect 60 🐚 . How many more 🐚 must she collect to meet her goal?

[   ] – [   ] = [   ]

She must collect [   ] more 🐚 .

– [   ]
  [   ]
  ———
  [   ]

⑨ Peter's goal was to collect 35 🐚 . How many more 🐚 had he collected ?

[   ] – [   ] = [   ]

He had collected [   ] more 🐚 .

– [   ]
  [   ]
  ———
  [   ]

⑩ How many 🐚 did the children collect in all?

[   ] + [   ] + [   ] = [   ]

They collected [   ] 🐚 in all.

+ [   ]
  [   ]
  ———
  [   ]

See how many animals are on each farm. Then use the table to answer the questions.

	Fred's Farm	Roy's Farm	Andy's Farm
🐔	37	29	27
🐄	16	28	23
🐴	15	16	49

⑪ Whose farm has the most 🐔 ?   _____'s farm

⑫ Whose farm has the most 🐄 ?   _____'s farm

⑬ Whose farm has the fewest 🐴 ?   _____'s farm

⑭ How many animals are there on Fred's farm?

_____ = _____   _____ animals

⑮ How many animals are there on Roy's farm?

_____ = _____   _____ animals

⑯ How many animals are there on Andy's farm?

_____ = _____   _____ animals

⑰ How many 🐔 are there on these three farms?

_____ = _____   _____ 🐔

⑱ How many 🐂 are there on these three farms?

_____ = _____ _____ 🐂

⑲ How many 🐴 are there on these three farms?

_____ = _____ _____ 🐴

⑳ How many 4-legged animals are there on Fred's farm?

_____ = _____ _____ animals

㉑ If Fred gives 12 🐔 to Roy, how many 🐔 are left?

_____ = _____ _____ 🐔

㉒ If Roy gets 12 🐔 from Fred, how many 🐔 does he have in all?

_____ = _____ _____ 🐔

㉓ If Andy buys 18 more 🐂 , how many 🐂 does he have in all?

_____ = _____ _____ 🐂

㉔ On Andy's farm, there are 16 male 🐴 . How many 🐴 on Andy's farm are female?

_____ = _____ _____ 🐴

㉕ On Andy's farm, there are 13 cocks. How many hens are there?

_____ = _____ _____ hens

Money

Write how much each item costs. Then answer the questions.

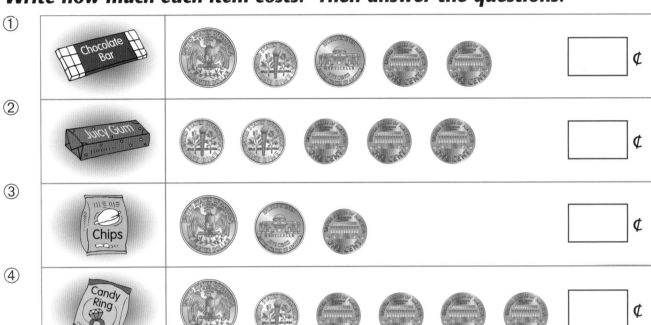

① Chocolate Bar — ☐ ¢

② Juicy Gum — ☐ ¢

③ Chips — ☐ ¢

④ Candy Ring — ☐ ¢

⑤ How many items cost more than 30¢? _____ items

⑥ Which is the most expensive item? _____

⑦ Which is the cheapest item? _____

⑧ Kathy buys 1 Chocolate Bar and 1 Juicy Gum. How much does she pay in all? She pays _____ ¢ in all.	42 + 23 _____
⑨ Lucy buys 1 Chips and 1 Candy Ring. How much does she pay in all? She pays _____ ¢ in all.	

228

⑩ Sean buys 1 [Chips] . How much change does he get from 50¢?

He gets _____ ¢ change.

⑪ Kim buys 1 [Candy Ring] . Sandy buys 1 [Juicy Gum] .

How much more does Kim pay?

Kim pays _____ ¢ more.

⑫ Jack buys 2 [Chocolate Bar] . How much does he pay in all?

He pays _____ ¢ in all.

⑬ The [Chips] is on sale. It costs 7¢ less. How much does it cost now?

It costs _____ ¢ now.

⑭ Cliff has 18¢. He wants to buy 1 [Juicy Gum] .

How much more money does he need?

He needs _____ ¢ more.

⑮ Amy has 24¢ and Brian has 18¢. They want to buy 1 item together. Which item with the highest price can they buy?

They can buy a _____ .

See how much each toy costs. Then complete the tables and answer the questions.

⑯

Number of 🪀	1	2	3
Cost	27 ¢	¢	¢

⑰

Number of 🎉	1	2	3
Cost			

⑱

Number of 🪀	1	2	3
Cost			

⑲ Jane buys a 🪀 and a 🎉. How much does she pay in all?

_____ = _____ _____ ¢ in all

⑳ Alexander buys a 🎉 and a 🪀. How much does he pay in all?

_____ = _____ _____ ¢ in all

㉑ Raymond pays 50¢ for a 🪀. How much change does he get?

_____ = _____ _____ ¢ change

Look at the toys on the previous page. Then answer the questions and check ✔ the fewest coins to match the answers.

㉒ Janet pays 50¢ for a ⬤ . How much change does she get?

_____ = _____   _____ ¢ change

㉓

㉔ Eddie pays 35¢ for a 🪀 . How much change does he get?

_____ = _____   _____ ¢ change

㉕

㉖ Tim buys 1 🪀 and 2 ⬤ . How much does he pay in all?

_____ = _____   _____ ¢ in all

㉗

㉘ Gary buys 1 ⬤ and 2 ⬤ . How much does he pay in all?

_____ = _____   _____ ¢ in all

㉙

Measurement

See how long each pencil is.   Then fill in the blanks.

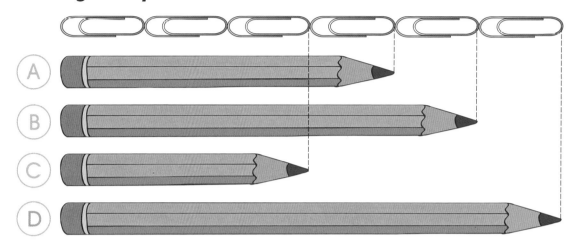

① Pencil A has the same length as _____ .

② Pencil B has the same length as _____ .

③ Pencil C has the same length as _____ .

④ Pencil D has the same length as _____ .

⑤ Put the pencils in order from the longest to the shortest.

_____ , _____ , _____ , _____

See how heavy each toy is.   Then fill in the blanks.

⑥ [bus] has the same weight as _____ [car] .

⑦ [robot] has the same weight as _____ [bus] .

⑧ Put the toys in order from the lightest to the heaviest.

_____ , _____ , _____

Write the time or draw the clock hands to show the times. Then answer the questions.

Mr. Smith's Meal Times

⑨ Breakfast — Half past seven

⑩ Lunch

⑪ Supper — Seven o'clock

⑫ Does Mr. Smith eat breakfast before or after seven o'clock? _____

⑬ Mr. Smith comes home at half past six. Is he early or late for supper? _____

Count and write the numbers.

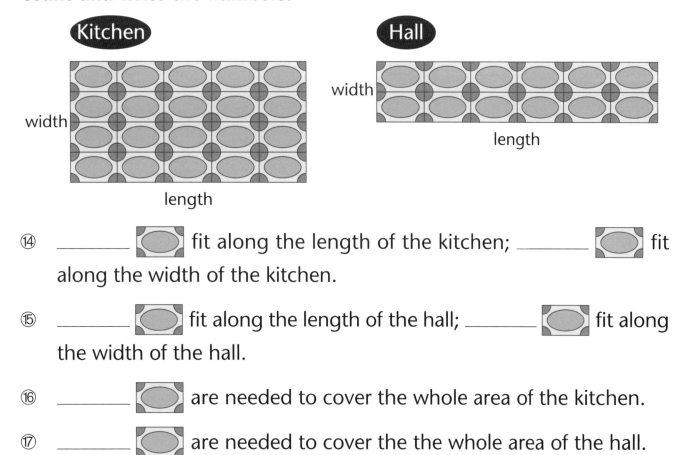

Kitchen

Hall

width

length

width

length

⑭ _____ 🔲 fit along the length of the kitchen; _____ 🔲 fit along the width of the kitchen.

⑮ _____ 🔲 fit along the length of the hall; _____ 🔲 fit along the width of the hall.

⑯ _____ 🔲 are needed to cover the whole area of the kitchen.

⑰ _____ 🔲 are needed to cover the the whole area of the hall.

 **Pictographs**

The children played their favorite sports last weekend. Look at the pictograph and check ✔ the correct answers.

Sports Played Last Weekend

① Which sport did the most children play?

  Ⓐ   Ⓑ   Ⓒ

② Which sport did the fewest children play?

  Ⓐ   Ⓑ   Ⓒ

③ How many children played ？

  Ⓐ 3   Ⓑ 4   Ⓒ 5

④ How many children played ？

  Ⓐ 3   Ⓑ 4   Ⓒ 5

⑤ How many children played or ？

  Ⓐ 7   Ⓑ 8   Ⓒ 9

⑥ How many more children played than ？

  Ⓐ 3   Ⓑ 2   Ⓒ 1

⑦ Which is the most possible season?

  Ⓐ Spring   Ⓑ Summer   Ⓒ Fall   Ⓓ Winter

Read the pictograph and answer the questions.

Number of Marbles Each Child Has

Joe	○ ○ ○ ○ ○ ○
Anita	○ ○
Britt	○ ○ ○ ○ ○
Paula	○ ○ ○ ○ ○ ○ ○ ○

⑧ Who has the most marbles? _____

⑨ Who has the fewest marbles? _____

⑩ Who has more marbles than Anita but fewer than Joe? _____

⑪ How many ○ do Joe and Britt have in all? _____ ○

⑫ How many ○ do Anita and Paula have in all? _____ ○

⑬ How many more ○ does Joe have than Anita? _____ ○

⑭ How many more ○ does Paula have than Britt? _____ ○

⑮ How many children have 6 or more marbles? _____ children

⑯ How many ○ do the children have in all? _____ ○

⑰ If Paula gives Britt 1 ○, how many ○ does Paula have now? _____ ○

⑱ If Britt gets 1 more ○, does she have more ○ than Joe? _____

Count how many toys Debbie has. Then color the pictograph and circle the correct answers.

⑲

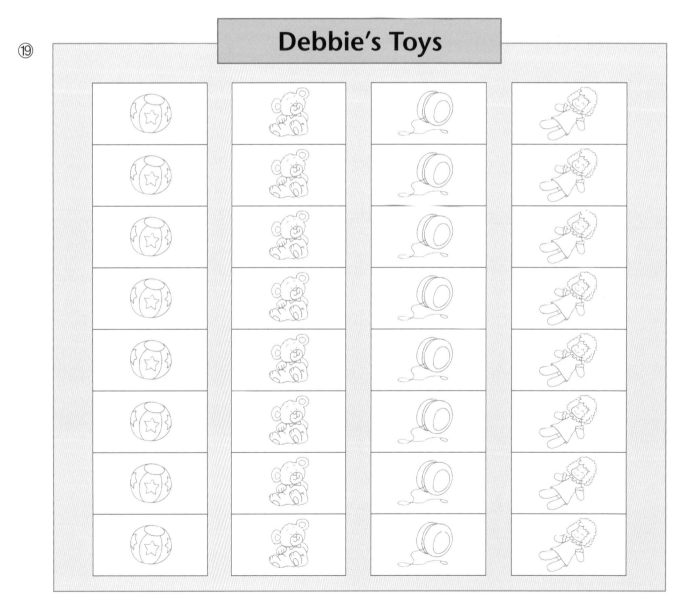

⑳ How many 🧸 does Debbie have?　　　6　　7　　8

㉑ How many 🔮 does Debbie have?　　　6　　7　　8

㉒ How many 🎎 and 🧸 does Debbie have?　　　12　　13　　14

㉓ How many 🪀 and 🔮 does Debbie have?　　　8　　9　　10

㉔ How many of Debbie's toys are not 🧸?　　12　　13　　14

㉕ Which kind of toy does Debbie have the most?　　🎎　🧸　🪀

㉖ Which kind of toy does Debbie have the fewest?　　🎎　🪀　🔮

㉗ How many more 🧸 than 🎎 does Debbie have?　　　3　　4　　5

㉘ How many toys does Debbie have in all?　　19　　20　　21

㉙ On Debbie's birthday, she gets 4 more 🎎. How many 🎎 does she have now?　　7　　8　　9

Probability

Look at the pictures. Then check ✔ the correct answers.

①

Is there a better chance that you will pick a or a ?

Ⓐ   Ⓑ

②

Is there a better chance that you will pick a or a ?

Ⓐ   Ⓑ

③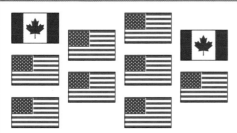

Is there a better chance that you will pick a or a ?

Ⓐ   Ⓑ

④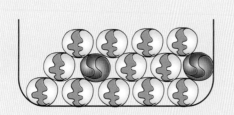

Is there a better chance that you will pick a or a ?

Ⓐ   Ⓑ

⑤ Which temperature is more likely in February in New York?

Ⓐ   Ⓑ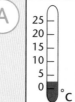

⑥ What time is more likely to have breakfast?

Ⓐ    Ⓑ

Look at the bag of marbles. Then check ✔ the correct answers.

⑦ Which word is the best to describe the chance of picking a green marble?

   (A) likely   (B) unlikely   (C) never

⑧ Which word is the best to describe the chance of picking a red marble?

   (A) likely   (B) unlikely   (C) never

⑨ Which word is the best to describe the chance of picking a black marble?

   (A) likely   (B) unlikely   (C) never   (D) maybe

⑩ What color are you most likely to pick from the bag?

   (A) yellow   (B) green   (C) red   (D) black

Look at the spinner. Then answer the questions.

⑪

a. Which word is the best to describe the chance of getting a Chips ?

   (A) never   (B) unlikely   (C) likely

b. Which word is the best to describe the chance of getting a 🍦 ?

   (A) never   (B) maybe   (C) likely

c. Which word is the best to describe the chance of getting a Chocolate Bar ?

   (A) never   (B) maybe   (C) unlikely

Count and write how much each child has. Then answer the questions.

① 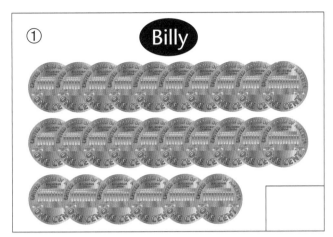 Billy

② 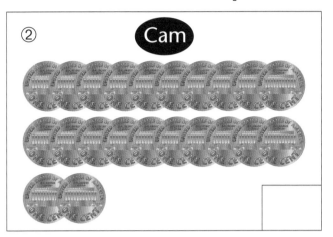 Cam

③ How much do Billy and Cam have in all?

[ ] + [ ] = [ ]

They have [ ] ¢ in all.

[ ]
+ [ ]
‾‾‾‾‾
[ ]

④ How much more does Billy have than Cam?

[ ] – [ ] = [ ]

Billy has [ ] ¢ more than Cam.

[ ]
– [ ]
‾‾‾‾‾
[ ]

⑤ Uncle Tom gives Billy 5¢. How much does Billy have now?

[ ] + [ ] = [ ]

Billy has [ ] ¢ now.

[ ]
+ [ ]
‾‾‾‾‾
[ ]

⑥ A 🍭 costs 7¢. Cam buys a 🍭 . How much has Cam left?

[ ] – [ ] = [ ]

Cam has [ ] ¢ left.

[ ]
– [ ]
‾‾‾‾‾
[ ]

See how many pizzas Mrs. Winter ordered for her class. Then answer the questions.

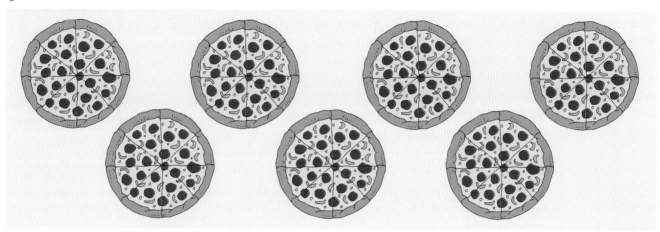

⑦ How many did Mrs. Winter order? _____

⑧ How many were there in each pizza? _____

⑨ How many of pizzas were there in all? _____

⑩ There were 24 children in Mrs. Winter's class. Each child ate 1 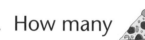. How many were left? _____

⑪ 15 of the children were girls. How many were boys? _____ boys

⑫ 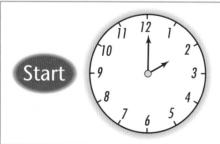 At what time did the party start? _____

⑬ 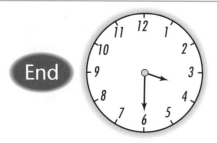 At what time did the party end? _____

241

Look at the ribbons. Write the letters to answer the questions.

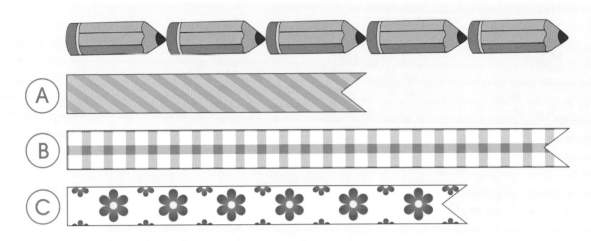

⑭ Which piece of ribbon is the longest?   Ribbon _____

⑮ Which piece of ribbon is the shortest?   Ribbon _____

⑯ Which piece of ribbon has the same length as
3 ✏ ?   Ribbon _____

⑰ Which piece of ribbon has the same length as
4 ✏ ?   Ribbon _____

Look at the number cards. Then circle the correct answers.

⑱ Is there a better chance that you will pick
a 1 or a 2 ?

⑲ Is there a better chance that you will pick
a 2 or a 3 ?

⑳ Which number card are you most likely
to pick?

242

Look at the pictograph. Then circle the correct answers.

Favorite Snacks in Mrs. Miller's Class

㉑ Which is the most popular snack?

㉒ Which is the least popular snack?

㉓ How many children like Candy ?   5   6   7

㉔ How many children like Chocolate Bar ?   5   6   7

㉕ How many more children like Chips
than Chocolate Bar ?   1   2   3

㉖ If 3 girls like Chips , how many boys
like Chips ?   2   3   4

See how many pets are in each shop. Then answer the questions.

	🐕	🐈	🐇
ABC PET SHOP	32	16	9
Bingo PET SHOP	14	28	13

㉗ How many pets are there in ABC Pet Shop?

_____ = _____   _____ pets

㉘ How many pets are there in Bingo Pet Shop?

_____ = _____   _____ pets

㉙ How many more dogs are in ABC Pet Shop than Bingo Pet Shop?

_____ = _____   _____ more dogs

㉚ How many more cats are in Bingo Pet Shop than in ABC Pet Shop?

_____ = _____   _____ more cats

㉛ How many rabbits are there in both pet shops?

_____ = _____   _____ rabbits

㉜ How many cats are there in both pet shops?

_____ = _____   _____ cats

㉝ If there are 13 white dogs in ABC Pet Shop, how many dogs in ABC Pet Shop are not white?

_____ = _____   _____ dogs

Parents' Guide

1. Comparing, Sorting, and Ordering

↦ Children may have difficulty in recognizing positions such as left and right. Parents should give them more practice in various situations so that they can internalize the concept.

↦ Ordering is a higher level of comparing. Parents can let children arrange objects under various rules.

2. Numbers 1 to 10

↦ Through games and daily experiences, children can learn and understand the difference between cardinal numbers (1, 2, 3 ...) and ordinal numbers (1st, 2nd, 3rd ...).

Example   5 children are buying snacks. Mary is the first one in the line.

↦ Practicing counting forward and backward helps children understand more about number sequencing.

↦ Simple words such as and/join (for addition), and take away/leave (for subtraction) can be used to guide children's calculation before they can use "+", "−", and "=" signs.

3. Addition and Subtraction

↦ To write vertical addition or subtraction, it is necessary to align all the numbers on the right-hand side.

Example   Vertical addition :

$$\begin{array}{r} 3 \\ + \ 1 \\ \hline 4 \end{array}$$ ↙ align on the right-hand side

Matching addition sentence:
3 + 1 = 4

Vertical subtraction :

$$\begin{array}{r} 5 \\ - \ 3 \\ \hline 2 \end{array}$$ ↙ align on the right-hand side

Matching subtraction sentence:
5 − 3 = 2

4. Numbers 11 to 20

↦ Counting on (forward) helps to find the sum faster.

Example   7 plus 5 means counting 5 forward from 7, and the sum of 7 + 5 is 12.

↦ Counting back (backward) helps to find the difference faster.

Example   13 minus 4 means counting 4 backward from 13, and the difference of 13 − 4 is 9.

↣ Any number plus or minus 0 equals itself.

Examples $7 + 0 = 7$ $9 - 0 = 9$

↣ Using tens may also help to find the sum or difference faster.

Examples $7 + 5 = 7 + 3 + 2$ $(5 = 3 + 2)$ $13 - 4 = 10 + 3 - 4$ $(13 = 10 + 3)$
$ = 10 + 2$ $ = 10 - 4 + 3$ (order changed)
$ = 12$ $ = 6 + 3$
$ = 9$

↣ Even if the order of addition changes, the answer remains the same.

Example $5 + 4 = 4 + 5 = 9$

5. Numbers 20 to 100

↣ It is easier for children to learn the numbers 20 to 100 by splitting them into two stages: 20 to 50, and 50 to 100

↣ Counting in groups of ten leads to the recognition of ones and tens.

Example

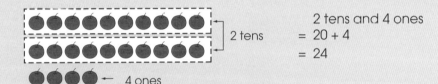

2 tens

2 tens and 4 ones
$= 20 + 4$
$= 24$

← 4 ones

↣ When comparing numbers, parents should remind children to compare the tens digit first, and if they are the same, compare the ones.

Examples   1.   Which one is greater, 25 or 51?
Compare the tens digit.

2|5
5|1

└ 5 is greater than 2

51 is greater than 25.

2.   Which one is greater, 38 or 32?
Compare the tens digit.   Compare the ones digit.

3|8   3|8
3|2   3|2

└ same   └ 8 is greater than 2.

38 is greater than 32.

6. More about Addition and Subtraction

↣ Before doing addition and subtraction, parents should make sure that children understand the meaning of place value. Children should understand that the digits in a 2-digit number represent groups of tens and groups of ones respectively.

Example   Sixty-five can be written as 65, six tens and five ones, and 60 + 5.

- To do vertical addition or subtraction:

  1st Align the numbers on the right-hand side.
  2nd Add or subtract the ones.
  3rd Add or subtract the tens.

  <u>Example</u>   16 + 23 =

	1st	2nd	3rd
	16	16	16
	+ 23	+ 23	+ 23
		9	39

- If the sum of the ones is 10, remind children to write 0 under the ones column, and bring 1 to the tens column.

  <u>Example</u>

13			13	
+ 27			+ 27	
4	✗		40	✓

- If the difference of the ones is 0, remind children to write 0 under the ones column.

  <u>Example</u>

32			32	
− 12			− 12	
2	✗		20	✓

- If the difference of the tens is 0, there is no need to write 0 under the tens column.

  <u>Example</u>

38			38	
− 30			− 30	
08	✗		8	✓

7. Measurement

- Parents should encourage children to describe dimensions with mathematical language, e.g. height, length, width etc., and use appropriate non-standard units such as erasers or books to measure different things. After that, parents can show them how to use standard units, e.g. inches and centimeters, to do measurement.

- To measure the length of an object, remind children to align "0" to one end of the object and get the length of the object from the other end.

  <u>Example</u>

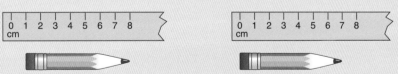

The pencil is 8 centimeters long. ✗   The pencil is 7 centimeters long. ✓

8. Time

↪   Children learn how to read the analog clock and tell the time by the hour and half hour. As they may have difficulty telling the exact position of the hour hand, parents should provide more guidance and practice for them.

Example

half past three ✗

The hour hand is halfway between 3 and 4.

half past three ✓

9. Money

↪   Children learn to name coins up to $0.25 and state the value of pennies, nickels, dimes, and quarters. Real coins can be used to play "buying things" with children to get them familiar with the value of each coin.

10. Shapes

↪   At this stage, children learn to recognize some 3-dimensional figures such as sphere, cylinder, cube, and cone, and some 2-dimensional figures such as circle, triangle, square, and rectangle. Parents may let children use building blocks and construction sets to consolidate their concepts of 3-dimensional and 2-dimensional figures.

↪   Symmetrical figures may have more than 1 line of symmetry.

Example

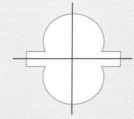

This symmetrical figure has 2 lines of symmetry.

11. Graphs

↪   Children need to know how to display and interpret data in a pictograph or solid column graph. Parents should encourage them to make comments about the graphs so that they can develop a better understanding of the data shown in the graphs.

1 Comparing Sizes

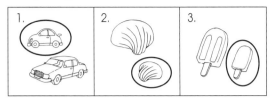

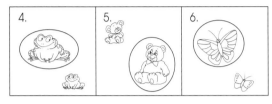

7- 9. (Suggested answers)

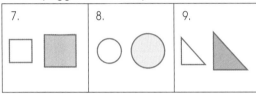

13 – 15. (Suggested answers)

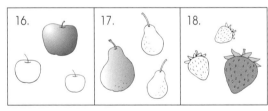

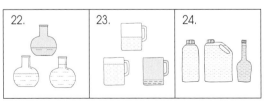

25 – 27.

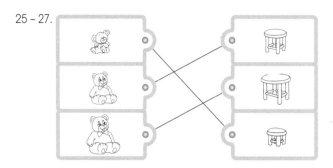

28. smaller   29. bigger   30. bigger
31. bigger   32. smaller   33. bigger
34. smallest   35. biggest

2 Comparing Heights and Lengths

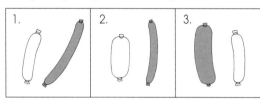

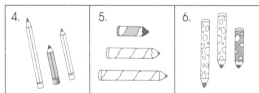

7- 12. (Suggested answers)

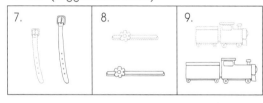

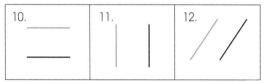

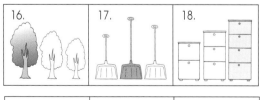

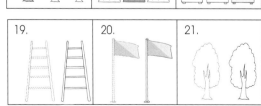

3 Comparing Shapes and Weights

1.

2.

3.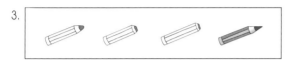

4.

5.

6.

7.

8.

9.

10.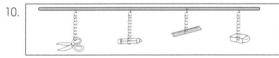

11. 12. 13.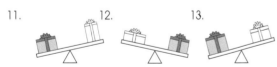

14. A   15. C   16. C

17. 18. 19. 20.

21. heavier   22. lighter   23. heavier
24. heavier   25. heavy   26. lighter

4 Comparing Positions

1. under   2. on   3. right
4. left   5. right   6. behind
7. in front of 8. inside   9. outside
10. right   11. left   12. right
13. right   14. in front of 15. behind
16. behind   17. over   18. under
19. over   20. under

21- 22.   23. inside

24- 25.   26. over

27- 28.    29. behind

30 – 39. (Suggested answers)
30 – 33.    34 - 36.

37 –39.

5 Matching and Arranging Objects

1. oranges
2. pears
3. apples or oranges or peaches
4. peaches
5.   6.
7. or   8. or
9.   10.   11.
12. fewer   13. more   14. fewer
15. C ; D ; A ; B   16. D ; B ; C ; A   17. D ; B ; A ; C ; E
18. D ; C ; A ; B ; E
19. bigger   20. bigger   21. B
22. C   23. B ; A ; C
24 – 25. (Suggested answers)
24.   25.

Midway Review

1a. Ⓐ Ⓑ Ⓒ Ⓓ

b. B ; C ; D ; A

2a. Ⓐ Ⓑ Ⓒ  Ⓓ

b. D ; C ; A ; B

3 – 6. (Suggested answers)

3.   4.

5.   6.

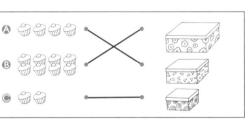

7. in front of	8. right	9. left
10. under	11. inside	12. bigger
13. more	14. A	15. B
16. B	17. A	18. right
19. left	20. left	21. behind
22. over	23. outside	24. inside
25. B	26. A	27. A
28. A		

29.

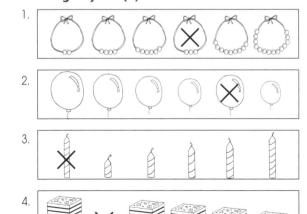

30. B   31. C   32. B ; A ; C

6 Ordering Objects (1)

1.
2.
3.
4.

5.

6.

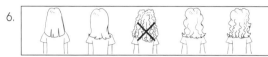

7. 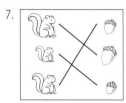   8.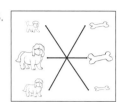

9. 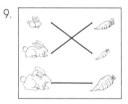   10.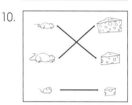

11. D ; C ; B ; A   12. D ; C ; B ; A

7 Ordering Objects (2)

1. A ; C ; D ; B	2. B ; A ; C ; D	3. B ; A ; C ; D
4. B ; D ; A ; C	5. D ; A ; B ; C	6. C ; D ; B ; A
7. B ; A ; D ; C	8. C ; B ; A ; D	9. A ; D ; C ; B
10. C ; A ; D ; B	11. B	12. A
13. B	14. C	15. C
16. C ; A ; B	17. B ; C ; A	

18.

19. Bert	20. Adam
21. Bert ; Dan ; Adam	22. Dan
23. Adam	24. Dan
25. Adam	26. Dan ; Bert ; Adam

8 Sorting Objects (1)

1.

2.

3.

4.

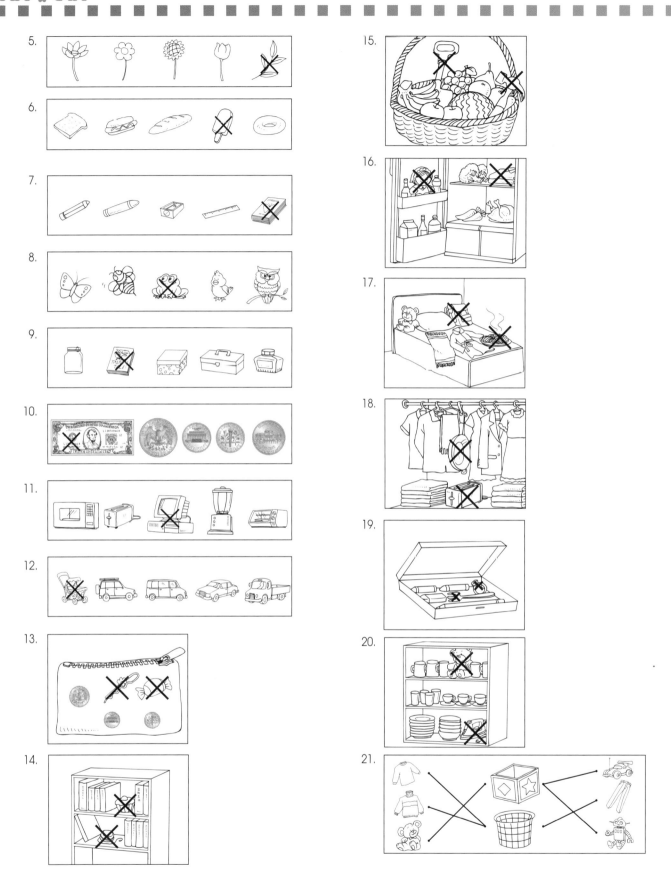

5.

6.

7.

8.

9.

10.

11.

12.

13.

14.

15.

16.

17.

18.

19.

20.

21.

22.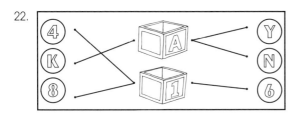

23.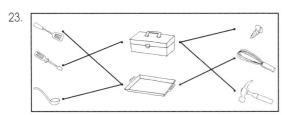

9 Sorting Objects (2)

1.

2.

3.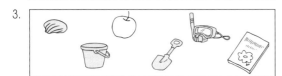

4.

5.

6.

7.

8.

9. can fly : B ; D   cannot fly : A ; C ; E
10. edible : A ; C ; D   not edible : B ; E
11. stationery : C ; D   not stationery : A ; B ; E
12. toys : B ; E   not toys : A ; C ; D
13. animals : B ; C ; E   plants : A ; D
14.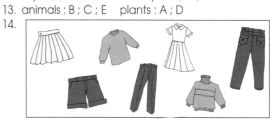

15.

16.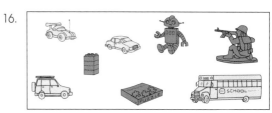

Final Review

1.

2.

3.

4.

5.

6.

7a.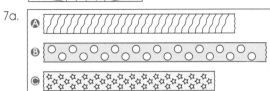

b. B ; A ; C

8.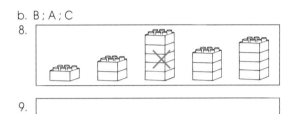

9.

10.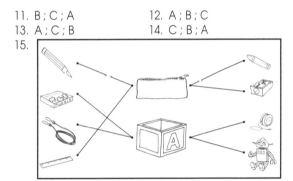

11. B ; C ; A   12. A ; B ; C
13. A ; C ; B   14. C ; B ; A
15.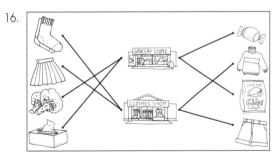

16.

17.

18.

19.

20.   21.

22.   23.

1 Addition and Subtraction of 1

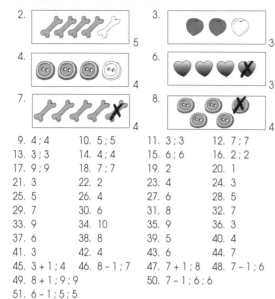

2. 5

3. 3

4. 4

6. 3

7. 4

8. 4

9. 4 ; 4	10. 5 ; 5	11. 3 ; 3	12. 7 ; 7
13. 3 ; 3	14. 4 ; 4	15. 6 ; 6	16. 2 ; 2
17. 9 ; 9	18. 7 ; 7	19. 2	20. 1
21. 3	22. 2	23. 4	24. 3
25. 5	26. 4	27. 6	28. 5
29. 7	30. 6	31. 8	32. 7
33. 9	34. 10	35. 9	36. 3
37. 6	38. 8	39. 5	40. 4
41. 3	42. 4	43. 6	44. 7
45. 3 + 1 ; 4	46. 8 – 1 ; 7	47. 7 + 1 ; 8	48. 7 – 1 ; 6
49. 8 + 1 ; 9 ; 9		50. 7 – 1 ; 6 ; 6	
51. 6 – 1 ; 5 ; 5			

Just for Fun

3 ; 4 ; 6 ; 7 ; 8 ; 10 ; 11 ; 12 ; 13 ; 15 ; 16 ; 17 ; 18 ; 19

2 Addition Facts to 6

2. 3 , 3 ; 6	3. 3 , 2 ; 5	4. 4 , 2 ; 6	5. 2 , 2 ; 4
6. 1 , 5 ; 6	7. 1 , 4 ; 5	8. 2 , 2 ; 4	9. 6
10. 5	11. 5	12. 3	13. 6
14. 4	15. 5	16. 6	17. 6
18. 2	19. 4	20. 5	21. 6
22. 4	23. 6	24. 6	25. 4
26. 3	27. 5	28. 6	29. 5
30. 5	31. 3	32. 6	33. 6
34. 4		35. 2 + 3 ; 3 + 2 ; 4 + 1	

36. 1 + 5 ; 3 + 3 ; 2 + 4 ; 5 + 1

37. ○○   ○○○   ○○○○   →
    2 , 4 ; 6

38. ○○   ○○○   ○○○○   →
    2 , 3 ; 5

39. 3 , 2 ; 5 ; 5   40. 4 , 2 ; 6 ; 6   41. 3 , 3 ; 6 ; 6

Just for Fun

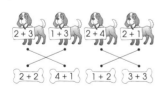

3 Subtraction Facts to 6

2. 4 , 2 ; 2	3. 6 , 2 ; 4	4. 5 , 2 ; 3	5. 5 , 3 ; 2
6. 5 , 4 ; 1	7. 3 , 2 ; 1	8. 6 , 3 ; 3	
9. 2	10. 5	11. 1	12. 1
13. 2	14. 1	15. 4	16. 3
17. 1	18. 2	19. 3	20. 3
21. 4	22. 2	23. 1	24. 2
25. 4	26. 2	27. 2	28. 2
29. 1	30. 3	31. 1	32. 3
33. 4	34. 1		

35. 5 – 3 ; 4 – 2 ; 3 – 1   36. 5 – 4 ; 3 – 2 ; 6 – 5

37. 4 , 2 ; 2	38. 5 , 2 ; 3
38. 6 , 3 ; 3	40. 6 , 2 ; 4
41. 4 , 3 ; 1	42. 3 , 2 ; 1

Just for Fun

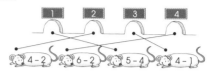

4 Addition and Subtraction of 0

1. 4	2. 0	3. 0	4. 3
5. 0	6. 4	7. 3	8. 5
9. 6	11. 6	12. 5	13. 5
14. 4	15. 4	16. 3	17. 3
18. 2	19. 2	20. 1	21. 1
22. 0	23. 0	24. 5	25. 4
26. 3	27. 1	28. 6	29. 3
30. 5	31. 6	32. 4	33. 2
34. 4	35. 2		

36.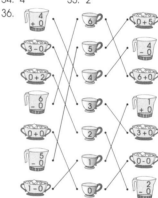

37. 2 ; 6	38. 5 ; 3 ; 1
39. 1 ; 3 ; 5	40. 6 ; 2 ; 4
41. 4 ; 4	42. 3 + 0 = 3 ; 3
43. 4 – 0 = 4 ; 4	44. 6 – 0 = 6 ; 6

Just for Fun

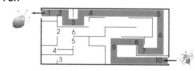

5 Addition and Subtraction Facts to 6

2. 6 – 1 ; 5	3. 3 + 3 ; 6	4. 4 – 2 ; 2
5. 5 – 2 ; 3	6. 2 + 3 ; 5	

7. 1	8. 4	9. 4	10. 3
11. 6	12. 3	13. 6	14. 3
15. 0	16. 2	17. 2	18. 3
19. 4	20. 5	21. 5	22. 1
23. 4	24. 1	25. 5	26. 1
27. 1	28. 6	29. 2	30. 2
31. 2	32. 4	33. 6	34. 5
35. 3	36. 4	37. 6	38. 3
39. 3	40. 2	41. 6	42. 5
43. 3	44. 1	45. 2	46. 4

47. 2 ; 2	48. 4 + 2 = 6 ; 6
49. 3 + 3 = 6 ; 6	50. 6 – 4 = 2 ; 2
51. 5 – 2 = 3 ; 3	52. 5 – 1 = 4 ; 4

Just For Fun

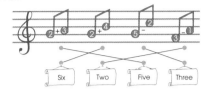

6 Addition Facts to 10

1. 9	2. 7 , 3 ; 10	3. 5 , 4 ; 9	4. 8 , 1 ; 9
5. 4 , 4 ; 8	6. 4 , 3 ; 7	7. 6 , 4 ; 10	
8. 9	9. 10	10. 10	11. 9
12. 9	13. 10	14. 9	15. 10
16. 8	17. 8	18. 7	19. 7
20. 10	21. 8	22. 9	23. 10
24. 8	25. 9	26. 8	27. 8
28. 9	29. 10	30. 7	31. 9
32. 7	33. 7		

35.

6 , 3

36.

7 , 2

37.

8 , 1

38.

9 , 0

39.

4 , 4

40.

5 , 3

41.

6 , 2

42.

7 , 1

43.

8 , 0

44.

4 , 3

45.

5 , 2

46.

6 , 1

47.

7 , 0

48.

49.

50. 8 , 0 ; 8 ; 8   51. 6 , 4 ; 10 ; 10
52. 6 , 3 ; 9 ; 9

Just for Fun

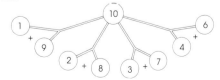

7 Subtraction Facts to 10

1. 6	2. 10 , 2 ; 8	3. 9 , 4 ; 5	4. 8 , 2 ; 6
5. 8 , 4 ; 4	6. 7 , 3 ; 4	7. 8 , 6 ; 2	
8. 6	9. 6	10. 6	11. 2
12. 5	13. 5	14. 5	15. 1
16. 1	17. 2	18. 2	19. 4
20. 4	21. 3	22. 3	23. 1
24. 2	25. 4	26. 1	27. 2
28. 3	29. 5	30. 8	31. 4
32. 10	33. 8		

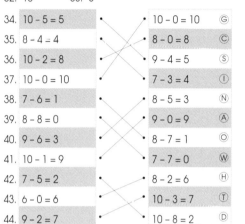

45. WASHINGTON D.C.

46.   47.

48. 7 , 4 ; 3 ; 3   49. 8 , 3 ; 5 ; 5   50. 10 , 2 ; 8 ; 8

Just for Fun

8 Addition and Subtraction Facts to 10

1. 9	2. 4 + 2 + 1 ; 7		3. 9 − 2 ; 7
4. 9 − 3 ; 6	5. 2 + 4 + 4 ; 10		6. 4 + 3 ; 7
7. 7	8. 2	9. 6	10. 10
11. 9	12. 3	13. 2	14. 7
15. 10	16. 1	17. 7	18. 7
19. 9	20. 10	21. 8	22. 9
23. 9	24. 8	25. 1	26. 3
27. 2	28. 5	29. 7	30. 8
31. 10	32. 9	33. 4	34. 9
35. 3	36. 10	37. 5	38. 2
39. 10	40. 10	41. 6	42. 4
43. 9	44. 6	45. 8	46. 5
47. 5	48. 4	49. 10	50. 3
51. 7	52. 6 ; 6		

53. 10   6
　　　　+ 4
　　　　——
　　　　10

54. 9   5
　　　　+ 4
　　　　——
　　　　9

55. 3 | 9 − 6 = 3 56. 7 | 2 + 4 + 1 = 7

Just for Fun

3 ; 4

Midway Review

1. 9 − 3 ; 6 2. 5 + 3 + 1 ; 9 3. 6 + 4 ; 10
4. 5 5. 6 6. 2 7. 2
8. 7 9. 1 10. 6 11. 7
12. 9 13. 7 14. 9 15. 1
16. 3 17. 8 18. 2 19. 7
20. 4 21. 8
22.
23.
24.
25.
26.
27. 10 ; 8 28. 4 ; 0 ; 2 29. − 30. +
31. 5 32. 2 33. 4 34. 3
35. 3 36. 4 37. 2 38. 5
39. − 40. + 41. + 42. −
43. − 44. + 45. − 46. +
47. − 48. − 49. + 50. +
51. 1 52. 3 53. 4 54. 4
55. 4 56. 3
57. 8 | 10 − 2 = 8 58. 3 | 6 − 3 = 3 59. 9 | 5 + 4 = 9
60. 8 | 2 + 6 = 8 61. 7 | 4 + 3 = 7 62. 4 | 8 − 4 = 4

9 Addition Facts to 15

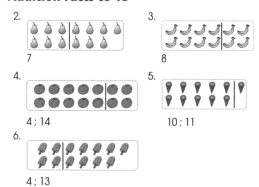
2. 7
3. 8
4. 4 ; 14
5. 10 ; 11
6. 4 ; 13

7. 15 8. 13 9. 14 10. 15
11. 14 12. 12 13. 12 14. 13
15. 14 16. 11 17. 11 18. 11
19. 14 20. 15 21. 13 22. 15
23. 12 24. 11 25. 12 26. 14
27. 13 28. 14 29. 15 30. 15
31. 15 32. 14 33. 11 34. 6
35. 10 36. 5 37. 9 38. 4
39. 8 40. 3 41. 7 42. 2
43.

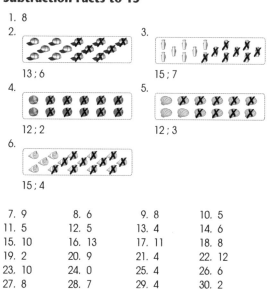
44.
45.
46.

47. 14 ; 14
48. 13 | 10 + 3 = 13 49. 12 | 12 + 0 = 12
50. 11 | 4 + 7 = 11

Just for Fun

5 ; 1

10 Subtraction Facts to 15

1. 8
2. 13 ; 6 3. 15 ; 7
4. 12 ; 2 5. 12 ; 3
6. 15 ; 4

7. 9 8. 6 9. 8 10. 5
11. 5 12. 5 13. 4 14. 6
15. 10 16. 13 17. 11 18. 8
19. 2 20. 9 21. 4 22. 12
23. 10 24. 0 25. 4 26. 6
27. 8 28. 7 29. 4 30. 2
31. 6 32. 5 33. 7 34. 8
35. 7 36. 9 37. 9 38. 2
39. 6 40. 10 41. 10 42. 3
43. 9

44. 6 ; 6

45. 5
```
    12
  -  7
     5
```
46. 8
```
    1 3
  -  5
     8
```

47. 9
```
    1 5
  -  6
     9
```

Just for Fun

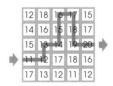

11 Addition and Subtraction Facts to 15

1. 9

3.

8

4.

13 ; 8

5.

12 ; 4

6.

4

7. 6   8. 13   9. 14   10. 4
11. 15   12. 6   13. 8   14. 11
15. 6   16. 14   17. 1   18. 15
19. 15   20. 9   21. 13   22. 5
23. 13   24. 2   25. 3   26. 7
27. 2   28. 15   29. 3   30. 14
31. 12   32. 6

33.

+	4	5	6
7	11	12	13
8	12	13	14
9	13	14	15

34.

13	14	15	-
6	7	8	7
5	6	7	8
4	5	6	9

35.
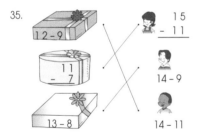

36.

37.

38. 14 ; 14

39. 4
```
    1 3
  -  9
     4
```

40. 4
```
    1 4
  - 10
     4
```
41. 11
```
     5
  +  6
    1 1
```

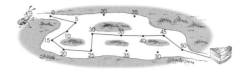

12 Addition Facts to 20

1. 9 , 8 ; 17   2. 14 , 5 ; 19   3. 11 , 6 ; 17
4. 15 , 3 ; 18   5. 13 , 7 ; 20   6. 10 , 6 ; 16
7. 20   8. 19   9. 19   10. 19
11. 19   12. 20   13. 19   14. 18
15. 17   16. 20   17. 17   18. 17
19. 17   20. 20   21. 19   22. 18
23. 20   24. 18   25. 16   26. 19
27. 17   28. 19   29. 20   30. 16
31. 20   32. 20

33. 15 + 3 = 18   n 13 + 3 = 16
34. 10 + 6 = 16   k 12 + 2 = 14
35. 9 + 5 = 14   r 16 + 2 = 18
36. 11 + 6 = 17   h 16 + 4 = 20
37. 12 + 8 = 20   c 16 + 1 = 17
38. 13 + 2 = 15   e 15 + 4 = 19
39. 16 + 3 = 19   d 14 + 1 = 15
40. 11 + 1 = 12   a 6 + 5 = 11
41. 9 + 4 = 13   f 10 + 2 = 12
42. 7 + 4 = 11   i 6 + 7 = 13

43. handkerchief   44. 10 + 10 ; 20 ; 20
45. 12 + 6 ; 18 ; 18   46. 8 + 8 ; 16 ; 16
47. 9 + 10 ; 19 ; 19   48. 13 + 4 ; 17 ; 17

Just for Fun

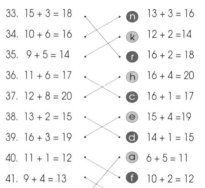

13 Subtraction Facts to 20

1. 8   2. 18 , 9 ; 9   3. 17 , 6 ; 11
4. 19 , 7 ; 12   5. 20 , 10 ; 10   6. 19 , 9 ; 10
7. 11   8. 7   9. 9   10. 15
11. 9   12. 6   13. 12   14. 14
15. 2   16. 13   17. 18   18. 3
19. 14   20. 6   21. 16   22. 6
23. 10   24. 12   25. 15   26. 9
27. 7   28. 6   29. 3   30. 4
31. 14   32. 13   33. 6   34. 7
35. 11   36. 5   37. 5   38. 1
39. 2   40. 5   41. 2   42. 7
43. 9   44. 12
45. 18 - 12 ; 6 ; 6   46. 17 - 9 ; 8 ; 8
47. 20 - 18 ; 2 ; 2   48. 16 - 5 ; 11 ; 11
49. 19 - 9 ; 10 ; 10

Just for Fun

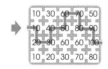

14 Addition and Subtraction Facts to 20

3. 7 ; 19   4. 18 ; 13

5. 20 ; 6   6. 9 ; 17

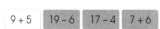

7. 14	8. 19	9. 19	10. 7
11. 3	12. 12	13. 3	14. 19
15. 4	16. 20	17. 20	18. 7
19. 20	20. 8	21. 17	22. 7
23. 20	24. 11	25. 3	26. 20
27. 4	28. 10	29. 16	30. 12
31. 20	32. 18		

33. 19 $12+7$ $20-1$ $14+4$ $13+6$

34. 16 $20-4$ $12+3$ $19-3$ $9+7$

35. 13 $9+5$ $19-6$ $17-4$ $7+6$

36. 15 $18-3$ $9+7$ $17-2$ $11+4$

37. 18 $18-0$ $20-2$ $10+8$ $12+5$

38. 11 $16-4$ $7+4$ $17-6$ $9+2$

39. 12 $8+4$ $19-7$ $6+5$ $16-4$

40. 5 ; 5

41. 10
$$\begin{array}{r} 18 \\ -\ 8 \\ \hline 10 \end{array}$$

42. 14
$$\begin{array}{r} 20 \\ -\ 6 \\ \hline 14 \end{array}$$

43. 19
$$\begin{array}{r} 13 \\ +\ 6 \\ \hline 19 \end{array}$$

44. 13
$$\begin{array}{r} 16 \\ -\ 3 \\ \hline 13 \end{array}$$

Just for Fun

65 ; 56 ; 48 ; 32 ; 29 ; 12 ; 7

15 More Addition and Subtraction

1a. 15	b. 16	c. 17	d. 18
e. 19			
2a. 17	b. 18	c. 19	d. 20
3a. 11	b. 12	c. 13	d. 14
4a. 9	b. 8	c. 7	d. 6
e. 5			
5a. 7	b. 8	c. 9	d. 10
e. 11			
6. 12			

7. 5 ; 15   8. 3 ; 13

9. 4 ; 14   10. 7 ; 17

11. 5 ; 15

12. 8

13. 2 ; 8   14. 3 ; 7

15. 4 ; 6   16. 3 ; 7

17. 2 ; 8

18. 14	19. 12	20. 18	21. 15
22. 16	23. 17	24. 19	25. 15

Just for Fun

16 Addition and Subtraction with Money

2. 6¢   3. 7¢   4. 8¢

5.

6.

7.

8.

9. 2   10. 5 , 4 ; 1   11. 7 , 7 ; 0

12. 10 , 5 ; 5   13. 10 , 6 ; 4   14. 3
15. 10 , 6 ; 4   16. 6 , 4 ; 2   17. 7 , 2 ; 5
18. 5 , 5 ; 0   19. A   20. D
21. B , C   22. B , D   23. C , D
24. A , B
25 - 27. Answers may vary.

25.

26.

27.

28. 3¢ + 4¢ ; 7¢ ; 7   29. 6¢ – 4¢ ; 2¢ ; 2
30. 5¢ + 1¢ ; 6¢ ; 6   31. 5¢ – 3¢ ; 2¢ ; 2
32. 1¢ + 4¢ + 5¢ ; 10¢ ; 10

Just for Fun

Final Review

1. 20   2. 11   3. 18   4. 15
5. 13   6. 16   7. 17   8. 10
9. 16   10. 10   11. 14   12. 19
13. 11 ; 8 ; 6 ; 9   14. 19 ; 18 ; 16 ; 20
15. 13 ; 10 ; 6 ; 12
16. 19   17. 13

18.
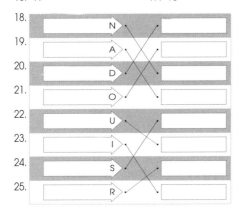

26. DINOSAUR
27. +   28. –   29. –   30. +
31. +   32. –   33. +   34. +
35. –   36. +   37. –   38. –
39. 10   40. 5   41. 8   42. 2
43. 5   44. 1   45. 12   46. 3
47. 4th ; 1st ; 2nd ; 3rd
48a. 13   b. 14   c. 15
49a. 8   b. 9   c. 10
50. 3 ; 13   51. 3 ; 13

52. 3 ; 7   53. 4 ; 6

54.

55.

56. 12   18   57. 18   6
            – 6   + 12
            ─────   ─────
              12   18

58. 5   10   59. 11   6
            – 5   + 5
            ─────   ─────
               5   11

60. 6   15   61. 2   9
            – 9   – 7
            ─────   ─────
               6   2

1 Comparing, Sorting, and Ordering

1. B, A
2. A, B
3. B, A
4. B, A
5. A, B
6. B, A
7. in front of
8. left
9. inside
10. under
11. B
12. A
13. A
14. C

15.
16.
17.
18.
19.
20.

21. ✓
22. ✓
23. ✓
24. ✓

25. 1, 3, 2
26. 2, 3, 1
27. 2, 1, 3
28. 3, 1, 2

Activity

2 Numbers 1 - 10

1. 5
2. 6
3. 8
4. 7
5, 6.

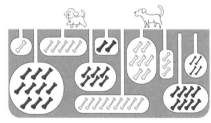

7. 5, 4, 3
8. 7, 8, 9
9. 9, 8, 7, 6, 5, 4, 3, 2
10.
11.
12.

13. 8
14. 3, 2, 5
15. 4, 2, 6
16. 5, 2, 7
17. 4, 5, 9
18. 3, 3, 6
19. 5, 1, 4
20. 8, 2, 6
21. 7, 2, 5
22. 8, 4, 4

Activity

3 Addition and Subtraction

1. 5
2. 4 + 3 = 7
3. 5 + 2 = 7
4. 6
5. 8
6. 9
7. 7
8. 7
9. 9
10. 10
11. 10
12. 10
13. 10
14. 10
15. 10
16. 7
17. 8
18. 6
19. 7
20. 9
21. 8
22. 10
23.

24. 3
25. 2, 3
26. 2
27. 8, 2
28. 3, 3
29. 1
30. 3
31. 4
32. 4
33. 1
34. 8
35. 4
36. 5
37. 6
38. 5
39. 7
40. 4
41. 2
42. 7
43. 4
44. 6
45. 4
46. 4

Activity

6 and 4   3 and 7
9 and 1   2 and 8

4 Numbers 11 - 20

1. 12, even
2. 17, odd
3. 13, odd
4. 16, even
5. 11, 13, 15, 17, 19
6. 14, 16, 18, 20
7. 12, 13, 14, 15, 16, 17
8. 19, 18, 17, 16, 15, 14
9. 18, 16, 14, 12, 10, 8
10. 7, 9, 11, 13, 15, 17
11. ✓
12. ✓
13. ✓
14.   15 = 10 + 5

15. 15 = 12 + 3

16. 15 = 8 + 7

17. 17 = 6 + 11

18. 17 = 8 + 9

19. 17 = 10 + 7

20. 17 = 4 + 13

21. 8 + 8 = 16	8 + 8 1 6	
22. 12 + 3 = 15	1 2 + 3 1 5	
23. 11 + 0 = 11	1 1 + 0 1 1	
24. 4 + 11 = 15	4 + 1 1 1 5	
25. 13 + 0 = 13	1 3 + 0 1 3	
26. 16 – 13 = 3	1 6 – 1 3 3	
27. 15 – 9 = 6	1 5 – 9 6	
28. 11 – 11 = 0	1 1 – 1 1 0	
29. 13 – 3 = 10	1 3 – 3 1 0	
30. 16 – 5 = 11	1 6 – 5 1 1	

31. 4   32. 2   33. 8
34. 4   35. 1   36. 2

Activity
1. 2   2. 7   3. 1
4. 14   5. 11   6. 6

5 Solids

1. A   2. D   3. C
4. B   5. E

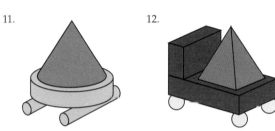

6. Sphere ✓
7. Prism ✓
8. Cylinder ✓
9. Pyramid ✓
10. Cone ✓

11.   12.

Activity

6 Solid Column Graphs

1. 7   2. 9   3.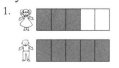
4. 2
5.

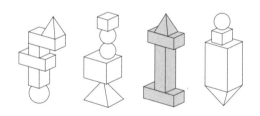

6. 6   7. 5   8. Orange
9. 1   10. Mrs. Lee   11. Mrs. Stanley
12. 2 squares 13. 1 square   14. 5
15. 5   16. 4   17. 14
18. Mark   19. David, 1   20. David
21. 4   22. 3   23. Jill
24. Mark   25. David, Nancy 26. 12

Activity
1.

2. 3   3. 5   4. 8

5. 2

7 Numbers 20 - 100

1. 71, 75, 77, 80, 82, 84, 86, 87, 90, 95, 96

2. 88   3. 76   4. 100, 92, 85, 73

5. 37, 39, 40, 42, 43   6. 26, 24, 23, 21, 20

7. 46, 47, 50, 51, 52   8. 91, 90, 89, 88, 86

9. 2 tens + 4 ones = 24   10. 3 tens + 8 ones = 38

11. 6 tens + 3 ones = 63   12. 7 tens + 4 ones = 74

13. fewer than 30, 22   14. fewer than 40, 34

15. fewer than 50, 45   16. more than 60, 62

17. 23, twenty-three

18. 30, thirty

19. 45, forty-five

20. 53, fifty-three

21. $30 + 5 = 35$

22. $20 + 3 = 23$

23. $60 + 0 = 60$

24. $50 + 4 = 54$

25.

26. 3 tens and 6 ones = 30 + 6

27. 4 tens and 9 ones = 40 + 9

28. 6 tens and 1 ones = 60 + 1

29. 7 tens and 5 ones = 70 + 5

30. 9 tens and 0 ones = 90 + 0

31. 0 tens and 9 ones = 0 + 9

32. 15, 20, 25, 30, 35, 45, 50, 55, 60

33. 30, 40, 50, 60

34. by 10's

35. 10   36. 25   37. 40

38. 10, 20   39. 8, 40

Activity

Midway Review

1. B, A   2. B, A

3.   4.

5.   6.

7.

8.

9.

10.

11.

12. $3 + 2 = 5$ 13. $7 - 5 = 2$

14. $3 + 2 + 3 = 8$

15. 13   16. 0   17. 15

18. 9   19. 7   20. 8

21. 11   22. 14   23. 19

24. 14   25. 11   26. 0

27. 18   28. 6   29. 16

30. 15   31. C   32. B

33. D   34. E   35. A

36. C   37. D   38. E

39.

40. 3   41. 12   42. 7

43. 5   44. 19   45. B

46. A   47. B   48. B

49. A   50. B   51. B

52. A   53. A   54. A

55. 52, 50, 43, 40, 26, 17   56. 41, 36, 30, 29, 20, 15

57. 30   58. 60   59. 9

60. 0   61. 80   62. 10
63. 0   64. 80   65. 5
66. 9   67. 9   68. 5
69. 70, 80, 90   70. 80, 85, 90   71. 19, 21, 23
72. 50, 55, 60   73. 74, 76, 78   74. 60, 62, 64

8 More about Addition and Subtraction

1. 43
```
  32
+ 11
  43
```

2.
```
  21
+ 46
  67
```

3.
```
   8
+ 70
  78
```

4. 78   5. 79   6. 67
7. 59

8. 63, 63
```
  34
+ 29
  63
```

9.
```
  28
+ 56
  84
```
10.
```
  37
+ 49
  86
```
11.
```
  12
+ 78
  90
```

12. 64   13. 75   14. 36
15. 40

16. 73
```
  33
  25
+ 15
  73
```

17.
```
  15
   8
+ 23
  46
```
18.
```
  16
  19
+ 36
  71
```

19.
```
  12
  23
+ 27
  62
```
20.
```
  32
   7
+ 26
  65
```
21.
```
  19
  28
+ 19
  66
```

22.
```
  16
  27
+ 38
  81
```
23.
```
  46
  28
+  9
  83
```
24.
```
  37
  27
+  7
  71
```

25. 48 – 15 = 33
```
  48
- 15
  33
```

26. 68 – 22 = 46
```
  68
- 22
  46
```

27. 22   28. 42   29. 23
30. 15   31. 20   32. 17
33. 2   34. 0   35. 6
36. 0

37. 13 + 16 = 29   29
```
  13
+ 16
  29
```

38. 36 + 21 + 16 = 73   73
```
  36
  21
+ 16
  73
```

39. 39 – 29 = 10   10
```
  39
- 29
  10
```

Activity

1. 44   2. 34   3. 56
4. 25   5. 47   6. 56
7. 25   8. 44   9. 34
10. 47
11.

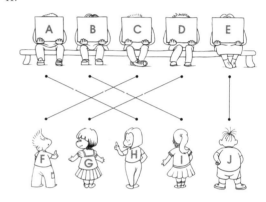

9 Measurement

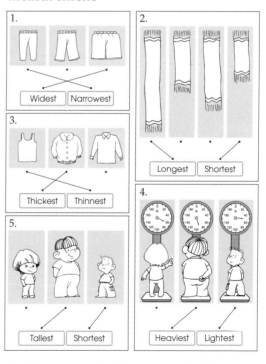

6. 4, 2   7. 6, 3   8. 8, 4
9. 10, 5   10. A   11. 2
12. 4

13.

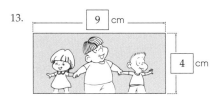

14. 10   15. 18   16. A
17. A   18. A   19. B
20. Estimate: individual answer   Count: 28
21. Estimate: individual answer   Count: 15
22. Estimate: individual answer   Count: 40

23.

24.

25.

26.

27.

28.

29. 5   30. 15

Activity

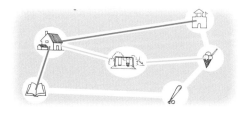

10 Time

1. 5   2. 9   3. 12
4. 7   5. 6   6. 11

7.   8.   9.

10. A   11. B   12. B
13. A   14. Monday   15. Wednesday
16. Friday   17. Sunday   18. 7

19 - 22. (Suggested answer)

January	February	March	April	May	June

July	August	September	October	November	December

23. A   24. B   25. B
26. C   27. 3, 1, 2, 4

Activity

			AUGUST			
Sunday	Monday	Tuesday	Wednesday	Thursday	Friday	Saturday
	1	2	3	4	5	6
7	8	9	10	11	12	13
14	15	16	17	18	19	20
21	22	23	24	25	26	27
28	29	30	31			

11 Money

1 - 4.

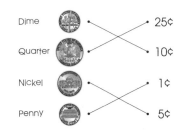

Dime   25¢
Quarter   10¢
Nickel   1¢
Penny   5¢

5. 3   6. 2   7. 2
8. 2   9. B   10. B
11. A   12. B

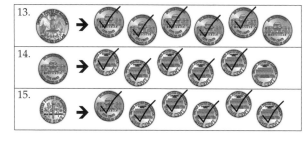

16. 47   17. 35
18. 33   19. 32
20.

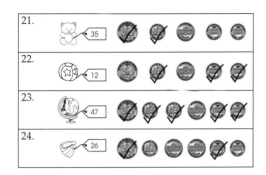

25. 54¢	2			4
26. 57¢	2		1	2
27. 64¢	2	1		4
28. 43¢	1	1	1	3

29.
```
   2 8
 + 2 5
   5 3
```
2

30.
```
   4 6
 +   5
   5 1
```
9

31.
```
   1 8
 + 3 7
   5 5
```
5

Activity

1. 5   2. 50

12 Shapes

1. B   2. B   3. A

4. B   5. A

6. 3   7. 2   8. 5
9. 3   10. 1
11. Yes   12. No   13. Yes
14. No   15. Yes   16. Yes

17.   18.

19.   20.

21.   22.   23.

24. Square

25. Triangle

26. Rectangle

27. Hexagon

28.   29.   30.   31.

32.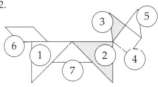

Activity

1. 5

2. a.   b.

3. a.

13 Pictographs

1. 8   2. 6   3. 4
4. 3   5. 2   6. 3
7. 21   8. 5

9   10. (ice cream)   11. (hamburger)

12. 17   13. 30

14.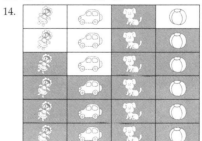

266

15. 1   16. 2   17. 10

18. 11   19. 19

20.
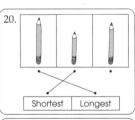
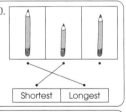
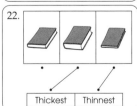

21. 6   22. 5   23. ♥

24. 16

Activity

1. 4   2. 3   3. Summer

Final Review

1. 87   2. 41   3. 41

4. 82   5. 33   6. 60

7. 41   8. 22   9. 80

10. 31   11. 0   12. 20

13. 48   14. 76

15. $39 + 0 + 25 = 64$
64

$$\begin{array}{r} 39 \\ 0 \\ +\ 25 \\ \hline 64 \end{array}$$

16. $16 + 20 + 40 = 76$
76

$$\begin{array}{r} 16 \\ 20 \\ +\ 40 \\ \hline 76 \end{array}$$

17. $43 + 28 + 0 = 71$
71

$$\begin{array}{r} 43 \\ 28 \\ +\ 0 \\ \hline 71 \end{array}$$

18. $76 - 71 = 5$
5

$$\begin{array}{r} 76 \\ -\ 71 \\ \hline 5 \end{array}$$

19.

20.

21.

22.

23.

24. 3   25. 1   26. 1

27. 14   28. 8   29. 8

30.

31. 12   32. 2

33. Monday, Tuesday, Thursday

34. June, July

35 - 38.

Weather / Season	Warmest	Coldest	Getting warmer	Getting colder
Spring			✔	
Summer	✔			
Fall				✔
Winter		✔		

39. 91   40. 82

41.

42 - 45.

🚗 35¢	1	1		
🪀 40¢	1	1	1	
👓 26¢	1			1
🔫 48¢	1	2		3

46.   47.   48.

49.

50.

51.

52. a. 6   b. 4   c. 3

    d. 8

53. a. hexagons

    b. circles

    c. squares, rectangles

1 Numbers 1 to 10

1. 8	2. 7	3. Helen
4. 10	5. 6	6. 7
7. Dan	8. Rick	9. 8
10. 9	11. 7	12. 5
13. 8	14. 6	15. 6
16. 2	17. 8	18. Jamie
19. Barry		

2 Addition and Subtraction to 10

1. 3	2. 6	3. 9
4. 4	5. Carol ; Ann	6. 9
7. 10	8. 7	9. 6
10. 3	11. 5	12. 7
13. 3	14. 4	15. 3
16. 9	17. 3	18. 2
19. 9	20. 1	21. 6
22. 10	23. 7	24. 10
25. 2	26. 4	27. 3
28. 10	29. 3 ; 6	30. 4
31. 2	32. 5	33. 2
34. 7	35. 2	36. 4
37. 7		

3 Addition and Subtraction to 20

1. 12	2. 16	3. 15
4. 9	5. 7	6. 13
7. 13	8. 11	9. 6
10. 8	11. 12	12. 14 ; 14

13. 20 ;
$$\begin{array}{r} 8 \\ + 12 \\ \hline 20 \end{array}$$
14. 6 ;
$$\begin{array}{r} 12 \\ - 6 \\ \hline 6 \end{array}$$

15. 4 ;
$$\begin{array}{r} 12 \\ - 8 \\ \hline 4 \end{array}$$
16. 7 ;
$$\begin{array}{r} 12 \\ - 5 \\ \hline 7 \end{array}$$

17. 18 ; 18
18. 11 – 7 = 4 ; 4
19. 17 – 5 = 12 ; 12
20. 12 – 5 = 7 ; 7
21. 13 + 7 = 20 ; 20
22. 13 – 7 = 6 ; 6
23. 3 + 11 = 14 ; 14
24. 11 – 3 = 8 ; 8
25. 6 + 6 + 6 = 18 ; 18
26. 20 – 18 = 2 ; 2
27. 12 – 4 = 8 ; 8
28. 12 + 5 = 17 ; 17

4 Shapes

1.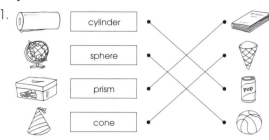

2. cube	3. prism
4. pyramid	5. cylinder ; ✔
6. ✔	7. ✔
8. ✔	9. ✗
10. ✗	11. 8
12. 7	13. 10
14. A	15. 2
16. rectangle	17. square
18. circle	19. triangle
20. hexagon	21. oval
22. 4 ; 4	23. 4 ; 4
24. 6 ; 6	25. 3 ; 3

26 – 28. (Suggested answers)

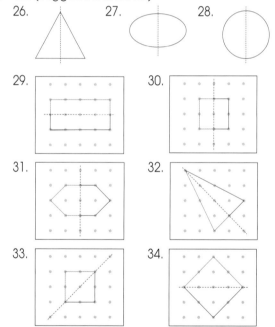

35-38. Estimate: Individual answer

35. 16	36. 14
37. 8	38. 8

5 Solid Column Graphs

1. B	2. C	3. A
4. A	5. C	6. Karen
7. Kim	8. 7	9. 5
10. 8	11. 12	12. 3
13. 20	14. 12	15. 4
16. 1	17. 3	18. 7

19.
Fishes in the Tank
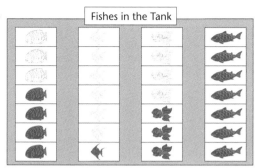

20. 4　　　　21. 6
22. 7　　　　23. 3
24. 4
25.
Animals in the Pet Shop
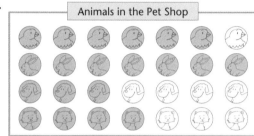

Midway Review

1. 10　　　2. 7　　　3. 4
4. 6　　　5. 9　　　6. 1
7.
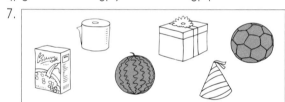
8. 7　　　9. 8　　　10. 4
11. 6　　　12. 11　　13. 14
14. 4　　　15. 15　　16. 10
17. 5　　　18. 11　　19. C
20. B　　　21. B　　22. B
23. A　　　24. C
25.
Judy's Collection
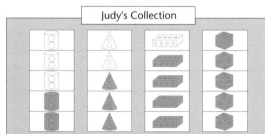
26.

circle
triangle
square
rectangle

27. 　　28.
29.

6　**Numbers 20 to 100**

1. 34　　　　2. 50
3. 46　　　　4. 29
5. B　　　　6. D
7. B ; C ; A ; D　　8. 60
9. 36　　　　10. 30
11. 45　　　　12. 62
13. 38　　　　14. Amy
15. Ivan　　　16. Amy ; Lily ; Ivan
17. 28　　　　18. 67
19. Dan　　　20. Mike
21. Brenda　　22. Brenda
23. Derek
24. Derek ; Mike ; Dan ; Brenda
25. 68 ; 53　　26. 80 ; 77
27. Dan
28. 55 ; 56 ; 57 ; 58 ; 59 ; 60
29. 69 ; 68 ; 67 ; 66 ; 65 ; 64
30. 35 ; 40 ; 45 ; 50 ; 55 ; 60
31. 84 ; 86 ; 88 ; 90 ; 92 ; 94
32. Mary　　　33. William
34. 45

7　**Addition and Subtraction to 50**

1. 12 ; 9　　　2. 15 ; 14
3. 12 + 15 = 27 ; 27　　4. 9 + 14 = 23 ; 23
5. 12 + 9 = 21 ; 21　　6. 15 + 14 = 29 ; 29
7. 21 + 29 = 50 ; 50　　8. 17
9. 29　　　10. 17 + 29 = 46 ; 46
11. 29 – 17 = 12 ; 12　　12. 17 + 15 = 32 ; 32
13. 29 + 15 = 44 ; 44　　14. 29 – 16 = 13 ; 13
15. 15 + 17 = 32 ; 32　　16. 11 + 14 = 25 ; 25
17. 18 + 19 = 37 ; 37　　18. 37 – 25 = 12 ; 12
19. 15 + 11 + 18 = 44 ; 44
20. 17 + 14 +19 = 50 ; 50
21. 21 – 17 = 4 ; 4　　22. 24 – 18 = 6 ; 6
23. 28 – 19 = 9 ; 9　　24. 21 + 24 = 45 ; 45
25. 21 + 28 = 49 ; 49　　26. 18 + 19 = 37 ; 37

8　**Addition and Subtraction to 100**

1. 41　　2. 25　　3. 33
4. 41 + 33 = 74 ; 74　　41
+ 33
74

5. 33 – 25 = 8 ; 8

```
  33
- 25
   8
```

6. 41 + 25 = 66 ; 66

```
  41
+ 25
  66
```

7. 41 – 25 = 16 ; 16

```
  41
- 25
  16
```

8. 60 – 33 = 27 ; 27

```
  60
- 33
  27
```

9. 41 – 35 = 6 ; 6

```
  41
- 35
   6
```

10. 41 + 25 + 33 = 99 ; 99

```
  41
  25
+ 33
  99
```

11. Fred   12. Roy   13. Fred

14. 37 + 16 + 15 = 68 ; 68

15. 29 + 28 + 16 = 73 ; 73

16. 27 + 23 + 49 = 99 ; 99

17. 37 + 29 + 27 = 93 ; 93

18. 16 + 28 + 23 = 67 ; 67

19. 15 + 16 + 49 = 80 ; 80

20. 16 + 15 = 31 ; 31

21. 37 – 12 = 25 ; 25

22. 29 + 12 = 41 ; 41

23. 23 + 18 = 41 ; 41

24. 49 – 16 = 33 ; 33

25. 27 – 13 = 14 ; 14

9   Money

1. 42   2. 23

3. 31   4. 39

5. 3   6. Chocolate Bar

7. Juicy Gum

8. 65 ; 65   9. 70 ;
```
  31
+ 39
  70
```

10. 19 ;
```
  50
- 31
  19
```
11. 16 ;
```
  39
- 23
  16
```

12. 84 ;
```
  42
+ 42
  84
```
13. 24 ;
```
  31
-  7
  24
```

14. 5 ;
```
  23
- 18
   5
```

15. chocolate bar ;
```
  24
+ 18
  42
```

16. 54 ; 81   17. 18¢ ; 36¢ ; 54¢

18. 24¢ ; 48¢ ; 72¢   19. 27 + 18 = 45 ; 45

20. 18 + 24 = 42 ; 42   21. 50 – 27 = 23 ; 23

22. 50 – 24 = 26 ; 26

23.

24. 35 – 27 = 8 ; 8

25.

26. 27 + 36 = 63 ; 63

27.

28. 18 + 48 = 66 ; 66

29.

10   Measurement

1. 4   2. 5

3. 3   4. 6

5. D ; B ; A ; C   6. 2

7. 3   8. A ; B ; C

9.   10. One o'clock

11.

12. After   13. Early

14. 5 ; 4   15. 6 ; 2

16. 20   17. 12

11   Pictographs

1. B   2. C   3. B

4. A   5. A   6. C

7. B   8. Paula   9. Anita

10. Britt   11. 11   12. 10

13. 4   14. 3   15. 2

16. 21   17. 7   18. No

270

19.

(grid of pictures)

20. 8   21. 6
22. 13   23. 8
24. 13
25. (teddy bear image)   26. (yo-yo image)

27. 3   28. 21
29. 9

12 Probability

1. A   2. A   3. B
4. A   5. A   6. B
7. A   8. B   9. C
10. B
11a. C   b. B   c. A

Final Review

1. 26   2. 22
3. 26 + 22 = 48 ; 48   2 6
                        + 2 2
                        ─────
                          4 8
4. 26 – 22 = 4 ; 4   2 6
                        – 2 2
                        ─────
                            4
5. 26 + 5 = 31 ; 31   2 6
                        +   5
                        ─────
                          3 1
6. 22 – 7 = 15 ; 15   2 2
                        –   7
                        ─────
                          1 5
7. 7   8. 8
9. 56   10. 32
11. 9   12. Two o'clock
13. Half past three
14. B   15. A
16. A   17. C
18. 1   19. 2
20. 1

21. (chips bag image)   22. (donut image)
23. 6   24. 5
25. 2   26. 4
27. 32 + 16 + 9 = 57 ; 57
28. 14 + 28 + 13 = 55 ; 55
29. 32 – 14 = 18 ; 18
30. 28 – 16 = 12 ; 12
31. 9 + 13 = 22 ; 22
32. 16 + 28 = 44 ; 44
33. 32 – 13 = 19 ; 19